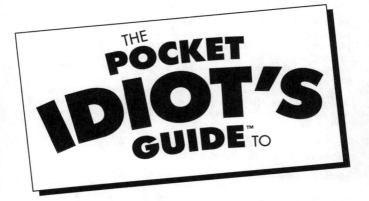

THE POCKET **IDIOT'S** GUIDE™ TO

German

by Alice Müller and Stephen Müller

alpha books

A Division of Macmillan General Reference
A Pearson Education Macmillan Company
1633 Broadway, New York, NY 10019-6785

©1999 Amaranth

THE POCKET IDIOT'S GUIDE TO name and design are registered trademarks of Macmillan Publishing, Inc.

Macmillan Publishing books may be purchased for business or sales promotional use. For information please write: Special Markets Department, Macmillan Publishing USA, 1633 Broadway, New York, NY 10019.

International Standard Book Number: 0-02-863177-3
Library of Congress Catalog Card Number: 98-83152

01 00 99   8 7 6 5 4 3 2 1

Interpretation of the printing code: the rightmost number of the first series of numbers is the year of the book's printing; the rightmost number of the second series of numbers is the number of the book's printing. For example, a printing code of 99-1 shows that the first printing occurred in 1999.

Printed in the United States of America

Publisher: Kathy Nebenhaus
Editorial Director: Gary M. Krebs
Managing Editor: Bob Shuman
Marketing Brand Manager: Felice Primeau
Acquisitions Editor: Jessica Faust
Development Editors: Phil Kitchel, Amy Zavatto
Assistant Editor: Georgette Blau
Book Producer: Amaranth
Production Editor: Jenaffer Brandt
Cover Designer: Mike Freeland
Photo Editor: Richard H. Fox
Illustrator: Floyd Hughes
Book Designer: Glenn Larsen
Indexer: John Jefferson
Layout/Proofreading: Carrie Allen, Marie Kristine P. Leonardo, Linda Quigley, Regina Rexrode, Terri Sheehan

Contents

Introduction

As you progress in your studies, you will find that German books, people, and customs are revealed in the German language in a way they never were in translation. If you plan a trip to a German-speaking country, even before you get on a plane, you should have the basic tools with which to decipher the code of the culture you're about to enter. What are these tools? Traveler's checks, an elementary knowledge of the German language, and an open mind. You're going to have to get the traveler's checks and the open mind on your own; we'll help you with the German language.

Extras to Help You Along

Besides the idiomatic expressions, helpful phrases, lists of vocabulary words, and down-to-earth grammar, this book has useful information provided in sidebars throughout the text. These elements are distinguished by the following icons:

Was haben Sie gesagt?

What did you say? These sidebars define grammatical terms and/or highlight or expand on some aspect of German grammar.

Achtung!

Achtung! boxes warn you of mistakes that are commonly made by those who are learning the German language and offer you advice about how to avoid these mistakes yourself.

Sagen Sie mal...

Tell me... These boxes provide quick glimpses into the German culture and/or give deeper insights into grammar, style, and usage in the German language.

Many foreign words have been adopted by the German language and still retain their foreign pronunciation. These words do not follow the German pronunciation guide included in this book.

Trademarks

All terms mentioned in this book that are known to be or are suspected of being trademarks or service marks have been appropriately capitalized. Alpha Books and Macmillan General Reference cannot attest to the accuracy of this information. Use of a term in this book should not be regarded as affecting the validity of any trademark or service mark.

Chapter 1

Let's Start at the Very Beginning

In This Chapter

➤ Learning by immersion

➤ Basic German rules of grammar

➤ Vowel sounds

Everybody knows that the best way to learn a new language is to totally immerse yourself in it. And, of course, to carry a phrase book with you for easy reference! *The Pocket Idiot's Guide to German* will tell you just as much as you'll need to know about German—enough to ask for a room with a Rhein-side view, make that ski trip to the Alps, host that German exchange student, or make that business trip to Berlin. With this book in hand, you'll feel empowered to go out and speak with confidence.

Learning by Immersion

Here are a few suggestions for immersing yourself up to your neck in German.

➤ You've got to know something of a language's grammatical structure to pick up shortcuts for quick and easy conversation. If grammar is tough for you in English, it isn't going to be any easier in German. Examine your goals, honestly evaluate your linguistic abilities, and set your pace accordingly.

➤ Invest in or borrow a good bilingual dictionary. A *Langenscheidt* standard dictionary costs approximately $19.

➤ Rent German movies.

➤ Tune your radio station to public service programs in German. Watch German shows on your TV. Go to public libraries and listen to language tapes. This will help you master German pronunciation.

➤ Read everything you can get your hands on. Children's books are a good place to start (Janosh, for example, is an author of simple and entertaining German children's books). Read the Brother's Grimm (*die Gebrüder Grimm*) side by side with the translation. Bedeck (*bedecken* in German, meaning "to cover") your coffee table with German newspapers: *Frankfurter Allge-meine* and *WAZ (Westdeutsche Allgemeine Zeitung)* and German magazines: *Focus, Die Bunte,* and *Der Stern,* to name a few.

Just in German

German words are pronounced exactly as they are spelled. You don't ever have to wonder if the "e" at the end of a word is silent, which it sometimes is and sometimes isn't in English. In German it's always pronounced. You'll also be glad to hear that the German alphabet consists of the same 26 letters as the English alphabet. There are, however, a few distinctly German language phenomena that you just can't do without.

Compendious Compounds

You're likely to come across German compound words everywhere you look. Because the possible combinations of nouns are practically unlimited, you can actually create your own compound words pretty much as you please by linking nouns together. The good news is that this is why the German language has been of such particular use to so many great thinkers. They have been able to express new concepts and ideas by making up brand new words. The bad news is, these compound words are not easily translatable. To express the meaning of the single word *Zeitgeist* in English, for example, you have to use the cumbersome and rather spiritless phrase, "spirit of the times."

Sagen Sie mal...

The word *das Menschengeschlecht (dAs men-shyn-guh-shleHt)* means mankind when taken as a whole; *Ge-schlecht*, however, can mean "genitals" on its own—a challenge for translators!

Stress in German

No, *stress* in German isn't what happens to you when your Mercedes breaks down on the *Autobahn*. A general rule for determining the stressed syllable in German is this: With words of more than one syllable, the emphasis is usually placed on the first syllable, as in the words **Blei**stift, **Schön**heit, and **Fra**ge.

Was haben Sie gesagt?

Stress The emphasis placed on one or more syllables of a word when you pronounce it. Stress in German

Foreign words such as *Hotel, Musik,* and *Natur* that have been assimilated into the German language do not follow German rules of stress or pronunciation.

Speaking in Tongues

Some people have no problem pronouncing new sounds in a foreign language. They were born rolling their Rs, and producing throaty gutturals. It doesn't matter if you can't make the exact German sound. Trying is the important thing. Strive for approximate perfection, and chances are, what you're trying to communicate will be understood.

It's Called an Umlaut

Ever notice those two dots that sometimes appear over vowels in German words? The umlaut is used to color, or alter, the sound of a vowel and to change a word's meaning—sometimes slightly, as in a plural form or sometimes more significantly, as in the comparison of an adjective.

Nouns Are in Caps

When you see half a dozen capital letters in the middle of a German sentence, they're not typos. One of the differences between written English and written German is that German nouns are always capitalized.

Which famous German writer and philosopher said that pleasure is simply the absence of pain?

Welcher berühmte deutsche Schriftsteller und Philosoph sagte, daß das Vergnügen schlicht die Abwesenheit von Kummer sei?

The answer is Arthur Schopenhauer.

Achtung!

An umlaut can be added only to *a*, *o*, or *u*. It can never be added to *e* or *i*.

Vowels, Vowels, Vowels

Three German vowels, "a," "o," and "u" can do a little cross-dressing. They're sometimes written with two dots above them—our versatile German umlaut.

➤ *Schon* means "already"; *schön* means "pretty" or "nice."

➤ *Ich trage* means "I carry" or "I wear"; *du trägst* means "you carry" or "you wear."

When a *vowel* takes an *umlaut* it becomes a *modified vowel*. In German, vowels and modified vowels can have long vowel sounds, which, as their name suggests, have a drawn out vowel sound (like the *o* sound in *snow*) or shorter vowel sounds, which have a shorter sound (like the *o* sound in *lot*).

Generally, a vowel is long when it is followed by an *h* as in *Mahl* (*mahl*). It is also long when it is doubled, as in *Meer* (*meyR*) and *Aal* (*ahl*), or when it is followed by a single consonant, as in *Wagen* (*vah-guhn*). The vowel *i* is made into a long vowel when it is followed by an *e*. In general, vowels are short when followed by two or more consonants.

Was haben Sie gesagt?

Vowel   *a, e, i, o,* and *u* are vowels

Umlaut   The term for the two dots that can be placed over the vowels

Modified Vowel   A vowel that takes an umlaut is referred to as a modofied vowel.

Who Are You Calling Dipthong?

Diphthongs begin with one vowel sound and end with a different vowel sound in the same syllable, as in the words "wine" and "bowel."

Was haben Sie gesagt?

Diphthongs   Combinations of vowels that begin with one vowel sound and end with a different vowel sound in the same syllable.

Your German Vowel Primer

In the following pronunciation guide, each vowel is given its own private section. We try to give you an idea of how vowel sounds are pronounced by providing you with an English equivalent.

A, Short and Long

German Letter(s)	Symbol	Pronunciation Guide
a (short)	*A*	Close to *o* in *modern*
a, aa, ah (long)	*ah*	Say *a* as in *father*

E, Short and Long

German Letter(s)	Symbol	Pronunciation Guide
e (short, stressed)	*e*	Say *e* as in *bed*
e (short, unstressed)	*uh*	Say *uh* as in *ago*
e, ee, eh (long)	*ey*	Close to the *ey* in *hey*

I, Short and Long

German Letter(s)	Symbol	Pronunciation Guide
i (short)	*i*	Say *i* as in *winter*
i, ie, ih (long)	*ee*	Say *ee* as in *beet*

O, Short and Long

German Letter(s)	Symbol	Pronunciation Guide
o (short)	*o*	Say *o* as in *lord*
o, oo, oh (long)	*oh*	Close to *o* in *snow*

U, Short and Long

German Letter(s)	Symbol	Pronunciation Guide
u (short)	*oo*	Close to *oo* in *shook*
u, uh (long)	*ew*	Say *ew* as in *stew*

Achtung!

Remember, the German *i* sounds like the English *e*.
Usually, the German *e* is soft, like the *e* in *effort*, or like
the *a* in *ago*.

Modified Vowels: Watch Your Umlauts!

In German, an umlaut changes the way a vowel is pronounced. Many German words are consistently spelled
with umlauts, but other words take an umlaut when they
undergo some change in pronunciation and meaning.
This guide treats each modified vowel separately.

Ä Is Not A

German Letter(s)	Symbol	Pronunciation Guide
ä (short)	*ä*	Say *ai* as in *fair*
ä, äh (long)	*äh*	Say *a* as in *fate*

Ö Is Not O

German Letter(s)	Symbol	Pronunciation Guide
ö (short)	*ö*	Close to *u* in *fur*
ö, öh (long)	*öh*	Close to *u* in *hurt*

Ü Is Not U

German Letter(s)	Symbol	Pronunciation Guide
ü, y (short)	*ü*	Close to *oo* in *food*
ü, üh, y (long)	*üh*	Close to *oo* in *food*, hold the sound for a longer interval of time

And Then There Were Diphthongs

Here are the diphthongs most frequently used in German. For other diphthongs, each vowel should be pronounced the same way it would be if pronounced separately: *Kollision (ko-lee-zeeohn), Familie (fah-mee-leeuh)*.

The Diphthongs EI and AI

German Letter(s)	Symbol	Pronunciation Guide
ei, ai	*ay*	Say *y* as in *cry*

Achtung!

Don't confuse *ie*, which is pronounced like *ee* in *feet*, with the diphthong *ei*, which is pronounced like the English word *eye*.

AU: The German OW!

German Letter(s)	Symbol	Pronunciation Guide
au	*ou*	Say *ou* as in *couch, mouse*

EU and ÄU: Oy-oy-oy!

German Letter(s)	Symbol	Pronunciation Guide
eu, äu	*oy*	Say *oy* as in *toy*

All right, you can breathe a sigh of relief now. We're through with the vowels. I you had a little trouble getting your mouth to do what you wanted to do it, don't worry. It will take you some time to get used to making sounds you've never made before. But remember: Practice makes perfect—or close to it!

Chapter 2

Concentrate on Consonants

In This Chapter

➤ German consonants

➤ Practice your pronunciation

The good news is, the sounds of German consonants are not going to be as unfamiliar as many of the sounds you tried in the previous chapter. In German, consonants are either pronounced like their English counterparts or are pronounced like other consonants in English. The only consonant sounds you won't encounter in English are the two sounds represented in this book by the symbol *H* (the *ch* in *ich*) and the symbol *CH* (the *ch* in *Loch* (lo*CH*)).

In written German, you'll also come across a new letter: the consonant β (pronounced, *es-tset*). It's a combination of the letters *s* and *z*, and is considered a single consonant. When people can't find the β key on their word processor, they often write the β as a double *ess* (*ss*). In either case, it should be pronounced like an *s*.

Hey! I Know These Letters!

There are many consonants that are pronounced the same way in German as they are in English. When you see them, just go ahead and pronounce them the way you would pronounce them if you came across them in English words.

German Letter(s)	Symbol	Pronunciation Guide
f,h,k,l,m,n,p,t,x	The same as English letters	Pronounced the same as in English

Was haben Sie gesagt?

Consonants All the letters in the alphabet other than *a, e, i, o,* and *u*.

Achtung!

The German *L* is not articulated in precisely the same place in the mouth as the English *L*. The English *L* is dark, formed with the tongue more relaxed. The German *L*— light, nearly as vibrant as the German *R*—is formed with the tip of the tongue just behind the upper front teeth.

The Plosive B, D, and G

Let's take a look at the letters *b*, *d*, and *g*. They are called *plosives* because of they way their sounds are articulated: with small explosions of air. At the beginning of a syllable, *b* is pronounced the same way as it is in English: *Bleistift* (*blay-shtift*), *braun* (*bRoun*), *aber* (*ah-buhR*). When *b* occurs at the end of a syllable, however, it is pronounced like a *p*: *Laub* (*loup*), *Korb* (*koRp*).

German Letter(s)	Symbol	Pronunciation Guide
b	*b*	Say *b* as in *big*
	p	Say *p* as in *pipe*

At the beginning of a syllable, the *d* is pronounced like an English *d*: *Dach* (*dACH*), *denken* (*den-kuhn*), or like the first *d* in *Deutschland* (*doytsh-lAnt*). At the end of a syllable, the *d* is pronounced like a *t*: *Leid* (*layt*) or like the last *d* in *Deutschland* (*doytsh-lAnt*).

German Letter(s)	Symbol	Pronunciation Guide
d	*d*	Say *d* as in *dog*
	t	Say *t* as in *tail*

At the beginning of a syllable, *g* is pronounced the same as it is in English: *Gott* (*got*). At the end of a syllable, *g* is pronounced like *k*: *Weg* (*veyk*). The consonant *g* has yet another pronunciation. In certain words, usually ones that have been assimilated into the German language from other languages such as French, pronounce the *g* as in: *Massage* (*mA-sah-juh*).

German Letter(s)	Symbol	Pronunciation Guide
g	*g*	Say *g* as in *God*
	k	Say *k* as in *kitchen*
	j	Say *j* as in *jeans*

Was haben Sie gesagt?

When the letters *ig* occur at the end of a word, they are pronounced the way *ich* is pronounced in the German word *ich*: *traurig* (*tRou-RiH*).

Friction with Fricatives

Fricatives are consonants articulated when the air stream coming up the throat and out of the mouth meets an obstacle, causing—you guessed it—friction. We have subdivided the German fricatives as follows:

Aw, Nuts: Z and Sometimes C

The *z* sound is made by combining the consonant sounds *t* and *s* into one sound: *zu* (*tsew*), *Zeug* (*tsoyk*), *Kreuz* (*kRoyts*).

German Letter(s)	Symbol	Pronunciation Guide
z	*ts*	Say *ts* as in *nuts*

In German, you probably won't run into a *c* that isn't followed by an *h* too often, but when you do, it should be pronounced *ts* whenever it occurs before *ä*, *e*, *i*, or *ö*: *CäsaR* (*tsäh-zahR*), or like the first *c* in *circa* (*tseeR-kah*). Otherwise, it should be pronounced like a *k*: *Creme* (*kReym*), *Computer* (*kom-pew-tuhR*), or like the last *c* in *circa* (*tseeR-kah*).

German Letter(s)	Symbol	Pronunciation Guide
c	*ts*	Say *ts* as in *nuts*
	k	Say *k* as in *keeper*

It's Kind of Like Gargling: CH, CHS, H, J

There's no exact English equivalent to the *ch* sound in German, but when you say words such as "hubrus" and "human," the sound you make when you pronounce the *h* at the very beginning of the word is very close to the correct pronunciation of the German *ch* in *ich* (this *ch* sound being one of the most difficult sounds, we might add, for English speakers learning to speak German). If you can draw out this *h* sound longer than you do in these two English words, you should have very little trouble pronouncing the following words accurately: *ich* (*iH*), *manchmal* (*mAnH-mahl*), *vielleicht* (*fee-layHt*).

The second *ch* sound is articulated at the same place in the back of the throat as *k*, but the tongue is lowered to allow air to come through. To approximate this sound (represented in this book by the symbol *CH*), make the altered *h* sound you just learned farther back in your throat—a little like gargling. Can you pronounce Johann Sebastian Bach's name correctly? Give this a shot: *Yoh-hAn zey-bAs-tee-ahn bahhhh* (gargle and hiss like a cat simultaneously at the end). Once you can do this, you have nothing to worry about: You've mastered this second *ch* sound.

In general, when *ch* occurs at the beginning of a word, it is pronounced like a *k*: *Chaos* (*kA-os*), *Charisma* (*kah-ris-mah*).

There are exceptions, however, as in *China*, where the *ch* is pronounced the same way it is in *ich*.

The *ch* has a fourth pronunciation: *sh*. This pronunciation is usually used only for foreign words that have been assimilated into the German language: *Chef* (*shef*), *Chance* (*shahn-suh*).

German Letter(s)	Symbol	Pronunciation Guide
ch	*H*	Close to *h* in *human*
	CH	No English equivalent
	k	Say *k* as in *character*
	sh	Say *sh* as in *shape*

You won't have any trouble at all with the *chs* sound. Say: *Fuchs* (*foox*), *Büchse* (*büxe*).

German Letter(s)	Symbol	Pronunciation Guide
chs	*x*	Say *x* as in *fox*

The *h* is silent when it follows a vowel to indicate that the vowel is long: *Stahl* (*shtahl*). In some cases, it is silent when it follows a *t*, as in *Theater* (*tey-ah-tuhR*). Otherwise, it is pronounced very much like the English *h*—just a little breathier. Think of an obscene phone caller breathing heavily on the other end of the line and try the following: *hallo* (*hA-loh*), *Weihe* (*vay-huh*).

German Letter(s)	Symbol	Pronunciation Guide
h	*h*	Say *h* as in *house*

Was haben Sie gesagt?

There is no English *th* sound in German. Either the *h* is silent, or both *t* and *h* are pronounced separately, as in the compound words *Stadthalle (shtAt–hA–luh)* and *Misthaufen (mist–hou–fuhn)*, both of which are "divided" by a glottal stop between the syllables.

Whenever you see a *j* in German, pronounce it like an English *y*: *Ja (yah)*, *Jaguar (yah-gew-ahR)*.

German Letter(s)	Symbol	Pronunciation Guide
j	*y*	Say *y* as in *yes*

Double Your Pleasure: KN, PS, QU

In English, the *k* is silent in words like "knight" and "knot." In German, however, both *k* and *n* are pronounced: *Kneipe (knay-puh52)*, *Knie (knee)*.

German Letter(s)	Symbol	Pronunciation Guide
kn	*kn*	Say *k* as in *kitchen* and *n* as in *now*

As in English, the consonants *ph* are pronounced *f*: *Photograph (foh-toh-gRahf)*, *Physik (füh-sik)*.

In the other consonant combinations in this chart, both letters are pronounced: *Pfeife (pfay-fuh)*, *Pferd (pfeRt)*, *Pseudonym (psoy-doh-nühm)*, *Schlinge (shlin-guh)*.

German Letter(s)	Symbol	Pronunciation Guide
pf	*pf*	No English equivalent
ph	*f*	Say *ph* as in *photo*
ps	*ps*	Say *ps* as in *psst*

The *qu* sound in German is a combination of the consonant sounds *k* and *v*: *Quantität* (*kvAn-tee-täht*), *Qual* (*kvahl*), *Quatsch* (*kvAtsh*).

German Letter(s)	Symbol	Pronunciation Guide
qu	*kv*	No English equivalent

VeRRy Interesting: The German R

Position your lips as if about to make the *r* sound, and then make the same gargling sound you made when making the German sound represented in this book by the symbol *CH*. The sound should come from somewhere in the back of your throat. The *r* sound can be soft, as in the words: *Vater* (*fah-tuhR*), *Wasser* (*vA-suhR*), or harder, as in the word: *reich* (*ReyH*). The distinction between these sounds is a subtle one. This book uses the same symbol (*R*) for both sounds.

German Letter(s)	Symbol	Pronunciation Guide
r	*R*	No English equivalent

Slide Those Consonants: S, β, SCH, ST, TSCH

The *s* is similar to the English *z*: *Sohn* (*zohn*), *Seife* (*zay-fuh*), *Rose* (*Roh-zuh*). At the end of a word, however, it is pronounced like the English *s*: *Maus* (*mous*), *Glas* (*glahs*).

German Letter(s)	Symbol	Pronunciation Guide
s	z	Say z as in *zero*
	s	Say s as in *house*

The letter β (*es-tset*) and the letters *ss* are both pronounced like an unvoiced *s*: *naβ* (*nAs*), *daβ* (*dAs*), *Maβe* (*mah-suh*), *Rasse* (*RA-suh*), *Klasse* (*klA-suh*), *müssen* (*müs-uhn*). In written German, the double *s* is used instead of β between two short vowels.

German Letter(s)	Symbol	Pronunciation Guide
β, ss	s	Say s as in *salt*

The consonants *sch* are pronounced *sh*: *Scheibe* (*shay-buh*), *Schatten* (*shA-tuhn*), *schieβen* (*shee-suhn*).

German Letter(s)	Symbol	Pronunciation Guide
sch	sh	Say sh as in *shape*

In German, *sp* is a combination of the *sh* sound in "shake" and the *p* sound in "pat." Try saying "ship" and leaving out the *i*. Now practice with these words: *Spiel* (*shpeel*), *Spanien* (*shpah-nee-uhn*).

The *st* sound is a combination of the *sh* sound in "shake" and the *t* sound in "take." Try saying "shot" without the *o* sound. Practice by saying the following words out loud: *steigen* (*shtay-guhn*), *Straβe* (*shtRah-suh*), *Stuhl* (*shtewl*).

The *st* sound is pronounced in some words or situations the same way as it is in English: *Meister* (*may-stuhR*), *Nest* (*nest*).

German Letter(s)	Symbol	Pronunciation Guide
sp	*shp*	No English equivalent
st	*sht*	Say *shot* without the *o*
	st	Say *st* as in *state*

Four consonants in a row! Don't panic. It's easier to read than it appears. *Tsch* is pronounced *tch*, as in the word "witch." See? A breeze, right?: *Matsch* (*mAtch*), *lutschen* (*loo-tchuhn*), *deutsch* (*doytch*).

German Letter(s)	Symbol	Pronunciation Guide
tsch	*tch*	Say *tch* as in *switch*

V & W: Isn't That a Car?

In most cases, the *v* is pronounced like an *f*: *Vater* (*fah-tuhR*), *Verkehr* (*feR-keyR*), *viel* (*feel*), but in some cases, particularly with words that have been assimilated into the German language from other languages such as French, the *v* is pronounced *v*: *Vampir* (*vAm-peeR*), *Vase* (*vah-zuh*).

German Letter(s)	Symbol	Pronunciation Guide
v	*f*	Pronounced as the *f* in *father*
	v	Sometimes as the *v* in *voice*

The *w* is pronounced like a *v*: *wichtig* (*viH-tiH*), *Wasser* (*vA-suhR*), *Wurst* (*vuRst*).

German Letter(s)	Symbol	Pronunciation Guide
w	*v*	Say *v* as in *vast*

Chapter 3

Getting Specific: Cognates, Gender, and Plurals

Chances are, you've been speaking German for years without even knowing it! *Kitsch, Wind, Mensch, Angst, Arm, blond, irrational, parallel*—the list of German words you already know is longer than you think. This is because there are many words in German that are similar to or exactly like their English counterparts. These words are called *cognates*.

Perfect Cognates: The German You Already Know

Table 3.1 lists by article *perfect cognates*—words that are exactly the same in English and German.

Table 3.1 Perfect Cognates

Adjectives	Nouns		
	Der	*Die*	*Das*
elegant *e-le-gAnt*	Bandit *bAn-deet*	Basis *bah-zis*	Folk *folk*
international *in-teR-nA-tsio-nahl*	Café *kA-fe*	Inspiration *een-spee-RA-tsion*	Museum *mew-zey-oom*
modern *moh-deRn*	Jaguar *yah-gooahr*	Olive *ohlee-vuh*	Organ *oR-gahn*
parallel *pA-rA-lehl*	Motor *moh-tohr*	Religion *rey-lee-geeohn*	Photo *foh-to*
wild *vilt*	President *pRey-zee-dent*	Tiger *tee-guhr*	System *süs-teym*

Was haben Sie gesagt?

Cognates Words in German that are similar to (near cognates) or exactly like (perfect cognates) their English counterparts.

Table 3.2 lists *near cognates*, words that are spelled almost—but not quite—the same in English and German. Although their spellings differ, their meanings are the same. Practice pronouncing the German words correctly. Don't forget to gargle those *CH*s and *R*s!

Table 3.2 Near Cognates

Adjectives	Nouns		
	Der	*Die*	*Das*
akademisch *AkA-dey-mish*	Aspekt *As-pekt*	Adresse *A-dRe-suh*	Adjektiv *Ad-yek-teef*
amerikanisch *Amey-Ree-kah-nish*	Bruder *bRew-duhR*	Bluse *blew-zuh*	Blut *blewt*
direkt *dee-Rekt*	Doktor *dook-tohr*	Gitarre *gee-tA-Ruh*	Glas *glahs*
frei *fRay*	Kaffee *kA-fey*	Kassette *kA-se-tuh*	Herz *heRts*
kalt *kAlt*	Ozean *ohtse-ahn*	Methode *me-toh-duh*	Papier *pah-peeR*
lang *lAng*	Preis *pRays*	Nationalität *nA-tseeo-näh-lee-tät*	Parfüm *pAR-füm*
perfekt *peR-fekt*	Stamm *shtAm*	Rhetorik *Reh-toh-Rik*	Programm *pRo-gRAm*
populär *poh-pew-lähR*	Supermarkt *zew-peR-maRkt*	Theorie *te-oh-Ree*	Salz *zAlts*
tropisch *tRo-pish*	Zickzack *tsik-tsAk*	Walnuß *wAl-noos*	Telefon *teh-luh-fohn*

Verb-al Affairs

It's time now to take a look at verb cognates in their infinitive forms. The *infinitive form* of a verb does not refer to a grammatical ghost that floats around in German sentences for all eternity. They end, and when they do, it is usually in *en*, as in the words *helfen* (*hel-fuhn*), *lernen* (*leR-nuhn*), and *machen* (*mA-CHuhn*). (In English, *to be* is an infinitive.) Table 3.3 is a list of verbs that are near cognates in their infinitive form.

Table 3.3 Verb Cognates

German	Pronunciation	English
beginnen	*buh-gi-nuhn*	to begin
bringen	*bRin-guhn*	to bring
finden	*fin-duhn*	to find
fühlen	*füh-luhn*	to feel
haben	*hah-buhn*	to have
helfen	*hel-fuhn*	to help
kommen	*ko-muhn*	to come
kosten	*kos-tuhn*	to cost
machen	*mA-Huhn*	to make
sagen	*zah-guhn*	to say
sitzen	*zi-tsuhn*	to sit
telefonieren	*tey-ley-foh-nee-Ruhn*	to telephone
trinken	*tRin-kuhn*	to drink

Was haben Sie gesagt?

Infinitive Form The unconjugated form of a verb. In German, the infinitive form of verbs end in *en*, or in some cases, simply *n*. Verbs are listed in the dictionary in the infinitive form.

Not All Words Are Cognates

No shortcut is without its pitfalls. Now that you've mastered the art of using words you already know to figure out words in German you didn't know you knew, we must warn you about false friends, or *falsche Freunde* (*fAl-shuh fRoyn-duh*). In language as in life, false friends are misleading. What are false friends in language? They are words spelled the same or almost the same in German and in English that have different meanings. Don't assume you already know the meaning of *every* German word that looks like an English word. It's not always that simple. Table 3.4 lists some common false friends.

Table 3.4   False Friends

English	Part of Speech	German	Part of Speech	Meaning
after	adverb	der* After *Af-tuhR*	noun	anus
also	adverb	also *Al-zoh*	conjunction	so, therefore
bald	adjective	bald *bAlt*	adverb	soon
blaze, blase	noun	die* Blase *blah-zuh*	noun	bladder, blister, or bubble
brief	adjective	der Brief *bReef*	noun	letter, official document
chef	noun	der Chef *shef*	noun	boss
closet	noun	das* Klosett *kloh-zet*	noun	toilet bowl
sympathetic	adjective	sympathisch *züm-pah-tish*	adjective	nice
kind	adjective	das Kind *kint*	noun	child
knack	noun	der Knacker *knA-kuhR*	noun	old fogey
lusty	adjective	lustig *loos-tik*	adjective	funny

continues

Table 3.4 Continued

English	Part of Speech	German	Part of Speech	Meaning
most	adjective	der Most *most*	noun	young wine
note	verb	die Note *noh-tuh*	noun	grade
see	verb	der See *zey*	noun	lake
sin	noun	der Sinn *zin*	noun	sense

*der is pronounced deyR, die is pronounced dee, and das is pronounced dAs.

Sex in German: All About Gender

If you've been reading this book carefully, you've probably already noticed that German nouns are preceded by three distinct definite articles: the masculine article *der* (*deyR*), the feminine article *die* (*dee*), or the neuter article *das* (*dAs*). All plural nouns are preceded by the plural article *die* (*dee*).

Determining gender can be tricky. Often, the natural gender of the noun and the grammatical gender of the definite article work the way you'd expect them to; *Herr* (*heR*), for example, the noun for "man," takes the masculine article *der* (*deyR*).

But more often, you can't get the article for a noun just by looking at it. (You can of course look the noun up in a dictionary, where masculine nouns are followed by *m.*, feminine nouns by *f.*, and neuter nouns by *n.*) Scholars have come up with many theories about why some nouns take certain definite articles, but the truth is, in German, there are no simple rules or explanations for determining gender. Why is the meat you eat at dinner neuter (*das Fleisch*), the potato feminine (*die Kartoffel*), and the cauliflower masculine (*der Rosenkohl*)? Your guess is as good as ours.

Other than learning the gender and the plural form of a noun along with the noun itself, there is no fail-safe way of ensuring that you know the correct gender of the German noun you are about to use in a sentence. The gender of a noun affects its relationship to other words in a sentence, and if you learn the definite articles along with the nouns, it will be easier for you to form sentences correctly later. There are a few tricks, however, for determining the gender of certain nouns as well as for altering the gender of certain other nouns, as in English when you change the word "waiter" to "waitress." We'll share them with you later in this chapter. Keep reading!

Achtung!

The noun marker for plural nouns (*die*) should not be confused with the feminine singular definite article (*die*). Only singular noun markers clearly show the gender of a noun.

Watch Your Noun Markers

Before you get into German nouns, there's one little obstacle you have to take a running leap over: The noun marker that precedes the noun. We use the term *noun marker* to refer to an article or adjective that tells us whether a noun is *masculine* (m.), *feminine* (f.), *neuter* (n.), *singular* (s.), or *plural* (p.). The most common noun markers, shown in Table 3.5, are definite articles expressing "the" and indefinite articles expressing "a," "an," or "one."

Table 3.5 Singular Noun Markers

	Masculine	Feminine	Neuter
the	der	die	das
one, a, an	ein	eine	ein

Singular Nouns

The nouns in Table 3.6 are easy to remember. There is an obvious correspondence between the grammatical gender of the noun marker and the natural gender of the noun.

Table 3.6 Gender–Obvious Nouns

Masculine Noun	Pronunciation	English
der Bruder	*deyR bRew-duhR*	the brother
der Cousin	*deyR koo-zin*	the cousin
der Freund	*deyR fRoynt*	the friend
der Vater	*deyR fah-tuhR*	the father
ein Mann	*ayn mAn*	the man
ein Sohn	*ayn zohn*	the son

Feminine Noun	Pronunciation	English
die Schwester	*dee shves-tuhR*	the sister
die Cousine	*dee koo-zee-nuh*	the cousin
die Freundin	*dee froyn-din*	the friend
die Mutter	*dee moo-tuhR*	the mother
eine Frau	*ay-nuh fRou*	the woman
eine Tochter	*ay-nuh toCH-tuhR*	the daughter

Even in a world where hardly anything is what it seems, there are still certain kinds of nouns whose gender you can determine even if you haven't memorized their definite articles. For example, nouns referring to male persons (*der Mann, der Sohn*), nouns of professions ending in *-er, -or, -ler* or *-ner* (*der Pastor, der Bäcker*), and most nouns referring to male animals of a species (*der Fuchs, der Löwe*) take the article *der*. Tables 3.7 through 3.9 group endings that will help you to identify the gender of nouns.

Table 3.7   Masculine Nouns

Masculine Endings	Example	Pronunciation	English Meaning
-ich	der Strich	*deyR shtRiH*	the line
-ig	der Honig	*deyR hoh-niH*	the honey
-ing	der Ring	*deyR Ring*	the ring
-ling	der Sträfling	*deyR shtRähf-ling*	the prisoner

Exception: *das Ding (dAs ding)*, the thing

Generally, two-syllable nouns ending in *-e* such as *Sonne (zo-nuh)*, and *Blume (blew-muh)*, take the feminine article *die*.

Table 3.8   Feminine Nouns

Feminine Endings	Example	Pronunciation	English Meaning
-ei	die Malerei	*dee mah-ley-Ray*	the painting
-heit	die Gesundheit	*dee gey-soont-hayt*	the health
-keit	die Leichtigkeit	*dee layH-tiH-kayt*	the lightness
-schaft	die Gesellschaft	*dee gey-zel-shAft*	the company
-ung	die Wanderung	*dee vAn-dey-Rung*	the walking tour

Das Berlin, das Deutschland, das Paris—countries, towns, and cities all take the neuter article *das*. So do the letters of the alphabet: *das A, das B, das C, das D*, and so on.

Table 3.9   Neuter Nouns

Neuter Endings	Example	Pronunciation	English Meaning
-lein	das Fräulein	*dAs fRoy-layn*	the young lady
-chen	das Hündchen	*dAs hünt-Huhn*	the doggy
-nis	das Ergebnis	*dAs eR-gep-nis*	the result
-tel	das Drittel	*dAs dRi-tuhl*	the third
-tum	das Eigentum	*dAs ay-guhn-tewm*	the property

Exceptions: der Irrtum (*deyR iR-tewm*), the error; der Reichtum (*deyR RayH-tewm*), the wealth; die Erlaubnis (*dee eR-loup-nis*), the permission; and die Erkenntnis (*dee eR-kent-nis*), the knowledge.

In German, there are certain nouns that never change their gender, regardless of whether they refer to a male or a female person or animal. Here are a few of them:

German	Pronunciation	English
das Kind	*dAs kint*	the child
das Model	*dAs moh-del*	the model
das Individuum	*dAs in-dee-vee-doo-oom*	the individual
der Flüchtling	*deyR flüHt-ling*	the refugee
das Opfer	*dAs op-feR*	the victim
das Genie	*dAs jey-nee*	the genius
die Person	*dee peR-zohn*	the person

In most cases, making nouns feminine is as easy as dropping the vowel (if the noun ends in a vowel), adding *-in* to the masculine noun, and, if the noun contains an *a*, an *o*, or a *u*, modifying this vowel: der Koch (*deyR koCH*), for example, becomes die Köchin (*dee kö-Hin*). Table 3.10 lists some common nouns that can undergo sex changes.

Table 3.10   Sex Changes

Masculine Ending	Feminine Ending	English Meaning
der Lehrer *deyR ley-Ruhr*	die Lehrer**in** *dee ley-Ruh-Rin*	the teacher
der Schüler *deyR shüh-luhr*	die Schüler**in** *dee shüh-luh-Rin*	the school boy/girl
der Arzt *deyR aRtst*	die Ärtzt**in** *dee äRts-tin*	the doctor
der Bauer *deyR bou-uhr*	die Bäuer**in** *dee boy-eyR-in*	the farmer
der Löwe *deyR löh-wuh*	die Löw**in** *dee löh-vin*	the lion

Making Plurals

In English, it's relatively easy to talk about more than one thing—usually, you just add an *s* to a word But there are plurals that stump learners of our language. How many childs do you have, or rather *children*? Are they silly little gooses, uh, *geese*? And what about those fishes in the deep blue sea—aren't they *fish*? In German plurals seem to be confusing too, but there is a method to the madness. In German, there are rules about forming plurals, in fact, an abundance of rules. This is what makes forming plurals in German such a challenge. For now, remember that when a noun becomes plural in German, the noun marker becomes plural with it. In German, the articles *der*, *die*, and *das* all become *die* in their plural form (see Table 3.11).

Table 3.11   Plural Noun Markers

	Masculine	Feminine	Neuter
the	die	die	die

More About Plurals

Everybody knows that if you've got more than one cat you've got cats (and a year's supply of kitty litter); if you buy more than one red Corvette you've got Corvettes (and a serious midlife crisis). In German, however, it's a little trickier. When nouns become plural in German, the noun either remains unchanged (*Mädchen*, for example, remains *Mädchen* in the plural) or takes *-e*, *-er*, *-n*, *-en*, or in a few cases *-s*. Many nouns undergo a vowel modification. There are rules for forming plurals in German, however, and many exceptions to these rules. The best way to be sure that you are forming the plural of a noun correctly is to memorize it along with the noun and the article. The following tables give you some basic rules on how to form plurals.

When the nouns in Table 3.12 and Table 3.13 become plural, they take either *-n* or *-en*. A majority of German nouns fall into this group, including most feminine nouns. The nouns in this group never take an umlaut in the plural, but if they already have one in the singular, it is retained.

When the nouns ending in *-e*, *-el*, and *-er* in Table 13.12 become plural, they take *-n*.

Table 3.12   Plural Nouns: Group I

German Noun Singular	German Noun Plural	English Meaning
das Auge *dAs ou-guh*	die Auge**n** *dee ou-guhn*	eye(s)
der Bauer *deyR bou-uhR*	die Bauer**n** *dee bou-uhRn*	farmer(s)
die Gruppe *dee gRoo-puh*	die Gruppe**n** *dee gRoo-puhn*	group(s)

German Noun Singular	German Noun Plural	English Meaning
die Kartoffel *dee kAR-to-fuhl*	die Kartoffeln *dee kAR-to-fuhln*	potato(es)
die Schüssel *dee shü-suhl*	die Schüsseln *dee shü-suhln*	bowl(s)

The majority of the nouns in Table 3.13 that take the ending -en in the plural are feminine nouns ending in -ung, -ion, -keit, -schaft, and -tät. All nouns referring to female persons or animals ending in -in double the *n* in the plural form.

Table 3.13 Plural Nouns: Group II

German Noun Singular	German Noun Plural	English Meaning
das Herz *dAs heRts*	die Herzen *dee heR-tsuhn*	heart(s)
das Ohr *dAs ohR*	die Ohren *dee oh-Ruhn*	ear(s)
die Freiheit *dee fRay-hayt*	die Freiheiten *dee fRay-hay-tuhn*	liberty(ies)
die Löwin *dee löh-vin*	die Löwinnen *dee löh-vi-nuhn*	the lioness(es)
die Mannschaft *dee mAn-shAft*	die Mannschaften *dee mAn-shAf-tuhn*	crew(s), team(s)
die Möglichkeit *dee mö-kliH-kayt*	die Möglichkeiten *dee mö-kliH-kay-tuhn*	possibility(ies)
die Qualität *dee kvah-lee-täht*	die Qualitäten *dee kvah-lee-täh-ten*	quality(ies)
die Religion *dee Rey-lee-gee-ohn*	die Religionen *dee Rey-lee-gee-oh-nuhn*	religion(s)
die Zeit *dee tsayt*	die Zeiten *dee tsay-tuhn*	time(s)
die Zeitung *dee tsay-toong*	die Zeitungen *dee tsay-toon-guhn*	newspaper(s)

The nouns in Table 3.14 take no ending in their plural form. Some of the masculine nouns in the group undergo a vowel modification, as do the only two feminine nouns in this group. The neuter nouns don't change.

Table 3.14   Plural Nouns: Group III

German Noun Singular	German Noun Plural	English Meaning
das Zimmer *dAs tsi-muhR*	die Zimmer *dee tsi-muhR*	the room(s)
der Garten *deyR gAR-tuhn*	die Gärten *dee gäR-tuhn*	the garden(s)
der Vater *deyR fah-tuhR*	die Väter *dee fäh-tuhR*	the father(s)
die Mutter *dee moo-tuhR*	die Mütter *dee mü-tuhR*	the mother(s)

When the nouns in Table 3.15 become plural, they take the ending -*e*. All neuter and feminine nouns that end in -*nis* double the *s* in the plural form.

Table 3.15   Plural Nouns: Group IV

German Noun Singular	German Noun Plural	English Meaning
das Ereignis *dAs eR-ayk-nis*	die Ereignisse *dee eR-ayk-ni-suh*	the event(s)
das Jahr *dAs yahR*	die Jahre *dee yah-Ruh*	the year(s)
der Brief *deyR bReef*	die Briefe *dee bRee-fuh*	the letter(s)
die Kenntnis *dee kent-nis*	die Kenntnisse *dee kent-ni-suh*	the knowledge
die Wand *dee vAnt*	die Wände *dee vän-duh*	the wall(s)

The plurals of the nouns in Table 3.16 end in *-er*. Wherever possible, vowels are modified. When they cannot be modified, as in the noun *das Bild*, (the vowels *e* and *i* never take an umlaut in German) the word takes the *-er* ending.

Table 3.16   Plural Nouns: Group V

German Noun Singular	German Noun Plural	English Meaning
das Bild *dAs bilt*	die Bild**er** *dee bil-duhR*	the painting(s)
das Buch *dAs bewCH*	die Büch**er** *dee bü-HuhR*	the book(s)
das Land *dAs lAnt*	die Länd**er** *dee län-duhR*	the country(ies)
der Mann *dyeR mAn*	die Männ**er** *dee mä-nuhR*	the man (men)

Sagen Sie mal...

Compound nouns take the plural form of the last noun. *Der Zahnarzt (deyR tsahn–ARtst)*, for example, is made up of the two words *der Zahn* and *der Arzt (deyR ARtst)*. Because *Arzt* comes last, it is the only part of the compound noun that becomes plural.

Always *die*

Some nouns in German are used only in their plural forms. These are worth noting, particularly because you don't have to worry about whether the articles preceding them are masculine, feminine, or neuter. They always take the plural article *die.*

German	English
die Ferien	vacation
die Geschwister	brothers and sisters
die Leute	people
die Eltern	parents

Was haben Sie gesagt?

A few nouns in German take an *-s* to form the plural. These are usually either words ending in "a," "i," or "u." Add "s" in the plural for nouns of foreign origin, such as *die Kamera* (*die Kameras*), *das Café* (*die Cafés*), *das Büro* (*die Büros*).

Chapter 4

Nouns on the Decline: A Case Study

Now that you have familiarized yourself with nouns, it's time to learn how to start forming sentences. In English, once you have the subject, the verb, and the direct object, this is an easy enough thing to do; you put the words in the right order and start talking. It doesn't work this way in German, however. Word order—the position of words in a sentence—isn't as crucial in German as it is in English. The reason for this is that in German, nouns, pronouns, articles, adjectives, and prepositions occur in four cases: nominative, accusative, dative, and genitive.

There Are Four Cases in German

You don't have to be Sherlock Holmes to figure out cases in German. Cases are the form nouns, pronouns, adjectives, and prepositions take in a sentence depending on their function. When we speak of cases and nouns, we are speaking of their articles, since it is primarily the article that comes before a noun that indicates its gender, number, and—you guessed it—case. There are four cases in German: nominative, accusative, dative, and genitive. Don't be put off. Basically, the nominative case indicates the subject of a sentence, the accusative case indicates the direct object of a sentence, and the dative case indicates the indirect object of a sentence.

Subject Object	Verb	Direct Object	Indirect
The girl	eats	the tail	of the fish

Was haben Sie gesagt?

Case The form nouns, pronouns, adjectives, and prepositions take depending on their function in a sentence.

The genitive case is used to show possession, as in the phrase "the fish's tail."

In German, cases enable you to vary the order of nouns and pronouns without changing the overall meaning of the sentence.

Das Mädchen ißt den Fisch.

Den Fisch ißt das Mädchen.

It may look to you like the fish is eating the girl in the second sentence. However, this is not true thanks to the cases taken by nouns *das Mädchen* (nom.) and *den Fisch* (acc.). Despite the position of the nouns, the noun markers remain the same in both sentences, clearly indicating that the fish is being eaten by the girl, and not that the girl is being eaten by the fish.

The Subject Is the Nominative Case

You begin with the nominative case. Nominative is the case of the *subject* of the sentence, that is, of the noun or pronoun performing the action (or undergoing the state of being) of the verb.

Nominative (Subject)	Verb
Ich (I)	trinke (drink)

The Accusative Case Goes with the Direct Object

The accusative case is the case you use with the direct object. The *direct object* refers to at whom or what the action of the verb is being directed. You also use the accusative case with time and measuring data that answers the questions how short, how soon, how often, how much, how old, and so on.

Nominative (Subject)	Verb	Accusative (Direct Object)
Er (he)	schickt (sends)	ein Paket (a package)

The Dative Case Goes with the Indirect Object

The dative case can be used instead of a possessive adjective with parts of the body and after certain verbs, prepositions, and adjectives. It is used primarily to indicate the indirect object, however. The *indirect object* is the object for whose benefit or in whose interest the action of the verb is being performed.

Nominative (Subject)	Verb	Dative (Indirect Object)	Accusative (Direct Object)
Er (he)	schickt (sends)	seinem Bruder (his brother)	ein Paket (a package)

The Genitive Case Takes Possession

The genitive case indicates possession.

Nominative (Subject)	Verb	Dative (Indirect Object)	Genitive (Possesive)	Acuusative (Diect Object)
Er (he)	schickt (sends)	der Frau (the wife)	seines Bruders (of his brother)	ein Paket (a package)

How Nouns Decline

Conjugation does not happen with nouns and pronouns. Only verbs can be conjugated. The term used to talk about the changes occurring in a word taking the four different cases is *declension*. Declension refers to the patterns of change followed by different groups of words in each of the four cases. When it comes to the declension of nouns in German, there are so many exceptions that at times it seems like there are as many ways of grouping and classifying German noun declensions as there are actual German nouns. For simplicity's sake, we are going to stick to three very basic declensions of German nouns: masculine, feminine, and neuter. Remember, this is only one way of grouping nouns and noun declensions.

Was haben Sie gesagt?

Declension The pattern of changes occurring in nouns, pronouns, articles, adjectives, and prepositions in each of the four different cases.

Sagen Sie mal...

Be sure that when you are looking up a noun, you look for it under its nominative singular form. This is the form under which nouns appear in the dictionary.

Declensions for Definite Articles

In German, there are four possible declensions for each definite article (remember, definite articles are used when you are speaking about a particular person or thing). The plural form of *der, die*, and *das* has its own separate declension.

Case	Masculine	Feminine	Neuter	Plural
Nom.	der	die	das	die
	deyR	*dee*	*dAs*	*dee*
Acc.	den	die	das	die
	deyn	*dee*	*dAs*	*dee*

continues

Case	Masculine	Feminine	Neuter	Plural
Dat.	dem *deym*	der *deyR*	dem *deym*	den *deyn*
Gen.	des *des*	der *deyR*	des *des*	der *deyR*

Declining Masculine Nouns

Most nouns have the ending *-s* in the genitive case. Some end with *-e* in the dative case.

Case	Noun	Pronunciation	Noun	Pronunciation
Nom.	der Fall	*deyR fAl*	der Vater	*deyR fah-tuhR*
Acc.	den Fall	*deyn fAl*	den Vater	*deyn fah-tuhR*
Dat.	dem Falle	*deym fA-luh*	dem Vater	*deym fah-tuhR*
Gen.	des Falles	*des fA-luhs*	des Vaters	*des fah-tuhRs*

A few masculine nouns end in *-n* in all cases except the nominative case.

Case	Noun	Pronunciation	Noun	Pronunciation
Nom.	der Student	*deyR shtew-dent*	der Junge	*deyR yoon-guh*
Acc.	den Studenten	*deyn shtew-den-tuhn*	den Jungen	*deyn yoon-guhn*
Dat.	dem Studenten	*deym shtew-den-tuhn*	dem Jungen	*deym yoon-guhn*
Gen.	des Studenten	*des shtew-den-tuhn*	des Jungen	*des yoon-guhn*

Declining Feminine Nouns

Are you ready for the good news? The declension of feminine nouns is a piece of cake. They remain unchanged when they are declined.

Case	Noun	Pronunciation	Noun	Pronunciation
Nom.	die Lust	*dee loost*	die Blume	*dee blew-muh*
Acc.	die Lust	*dee loost*	die Blume	*dee blew-muh*
Dat.	der Lust	*deyR loost*	der Blume	*deyR blew-muh*
Gen.	der Lust	*deyR loost*	der Blume	*deyR blew-muh*

Declining Neuter Nouns

Neuter nouns end in *-s* in the genitive case. Some take the ending *-e* in the dative case.

Case	Noun	Pronunciation	Noun	Pronunciation
Nom.	das Jahr	*dAs yahR*	das Licht	*dAs liHt*
Acc.	das Jahr	*dAs yahR*	das Licht	*dAs liHt*
Dat.	dem Jahre	*deym yah-Ruh*	dem Licht	*deym liHt*
Gen.	des Jahres	*des yah-Ruhs*	des Lichts	*des liHts*

Declining Plurals

Other than the dative case, all nouns in the plural form end in *-er*. Nouns in the dative case end in *-n*.

Case	Noun	Pronunciation	Noun	Pronunciation
Nom.	die Väter	*dee fäh-tuhR*	die Lichter	*dee liH-tuhR*
Acc.	die Väter	*dee fäh-tuhR*	die Lichter	*dee liH-tuhR*
Dat.	den Vätern	*deyn fäh-tuhRn*	den Lichtern	*deyn liH-tuhRn*
Gen.	der Väter	*deyR fäh-tuhR*	der Lichter	*deyR liH-tuhR*

Plural nouns that end in *-n* or *-s* remain unchanged.

Case	Noun	Pronunciation	Noun	Pronunciation
Nom.	die Blumen	*dee blew-muhn*	die Hotels	*dee hoh-tels*
Acc.	die Blumen	*dee blew-muhn*	die Hotels	*dee hoh-tels*
Dat.	den Blumen	*deyR blew-muhn*	den Hotels	*deyn hoh-tels*
Gen.	der Blumen	*deyR blew-muhn*	der Hotels	*deyR hoh-tels*

And Then There's the Indefinite Article...

The English equivalent for the indefinite article is "a" or "an." *Indefinite articles* are used when you are speaking about a noun in general, and not about a specific noun. There are only three possible declensions for the indefinite article, since indefinite articles do not occur in the plural.

Case	Masculine	Feminine	Neuter	Plural
Nom.	ein *ayn*	eine *ay-nuh*	ein *ayn*	none
Acc.	einen *ay-nuhn*	eine *ay-nuh*	ein *ayn*	none
Dat.	einem *ay-nuhm*	einer *ay-nuhr*	einem *ay-nuhm*	none
Gen.	eines *ay-nuhs*	einer *ay-nuhr*	eines *ay-nuhs*	none

Achtung!

In some cases, the endings of nouns change along with their definite article. There are three possible endings for nouns. These are -(e)s, -(e)n and -e.

Finding the Subject Pronoun

Before you can form sentences with verbs in German, you will have to know something about subject pronouns. A subject pronoun is, as its name suggests, the subject of a sentence; the verb must agree with it (grammatically speaking, that is, in person and number—we all know verbs don't have opinions of their own). The German subject pronouns in Table 4.1 have a person (first person is "I," second person is "you," third person is "he," "she," or "it," etc.) just as subject pronouns do in English, and in number (singular or plural).

Table 4.1 Subject Pronouns

Case	Singular	English	Plural	English
First	ich *iH*	I	wir *veer*	we
Second	du *dew*	you	ihr *eer*	you
Formal	Sie *zee*	you		
Third	er, sie, es *eR, zee, es*	he, she, it	sie *zee*	they

Was haben Sie gesagt?

Indefinite article   Articles used when you are speaking about a noun in general, and not about a specific noun.

Being Polite in German: Du versus Sie

In German, however, *Sie* (the polite form for you) is still
very much a part of the German vocabulary. Generally, *Sie*
is used with people you don't know, or to indicate respect.
Du, the informal "you," is used more casually—with those
who are your peers or with those you know well.

Informal:	Wie heißt du?	What's your name?
	vee hayst dew	
Formal:	Wie heißen Sie?	What's your name?
	vee hay-suhn zee	

You can also use pronouns to replace the name of a common noun referring to a place, thing, or idea; note from
the examples that the gender of the pronoun must corre-
spond to the gender of the noun:

Noun	Pronunciation	Pronoun	Meaning
das Restaurant	*dAs Res-tou-Rant*	es	the restaurant
die Bank	*dee bAnk*	sie	the bank
das Café und das Kino	*dAs kah-fey oont dAs kee-noh*	sie	the café and the movie theater
der Hafen und das Schiff	*deyR ha-fuhn oond dAs shif*	sie	the harbor and the ship
die Straße und die Kirche	*dee ShtRah-suh oond dee KeeR-Huh*	sie	the street and the church
das Geschäft und die Schuhe	*dAs guh-shäft oond dee shew-huh*	sie	the store and the shoes

Achtung!

Be careful when you use the pronoun "sie." Don't mix up the singular *sie* (she) with the plural *sie* (they). The verb indicates whether the pronoun *sie* is being used as third person singular or third person plural. The formal *Sie* (you) is always capitalized.

Chapter 5

Verbs: Conjugating the Weak and the Strong

In This Chapter

➤ Understanding subject pronouns

➤ Conjugating weak and strong verbs

➤ Using common weak and strong verbs

➤ Learning how to ask questions

Verbs, the Arnold Schwarzeneggers of the language set, convey action in a sentence. To communicate it is crucial to develop a basic understanding of verbs. In this chapter, you'll be introduced to weak and strong verbs.

Finding the Subject

To express what people want to do, you need verbs, and verbs, of course, require a subject:

➤ *You* want to take quiet, relaxing strolls through churches and parks.

➤ *The woman* wants to spend three days shopping in Zürich.

When a sentence takes the *imperative form*, the form of a command, the subject (you) is understood:

➤ Go shopping.

Subjects can be either nouns or pronouns that replace nouns:

➤ *The man* ate the entire chicken.

➤ *He* ate the entire chicken.

Was haben Sie gesagt?

Unlike German nouns, which are capitalized no matter where they appear in a sentence, most pronouns take a capital letter only when they begin a sentence. The only exception to this rule is the pronoun *Sie* (the polite form for *du* and *ihr*), which is capitalized no matter where it appears in a sentence.

And the Verb Is...

It's easier to understand how a plane takes off if you know something about its parts. It's the same with verbs. Here are some basic things you should know about verbs before you start using them.

Verbs Have Stems, Too

So, what do flowers and verbs have in common? The answer is, stems. The stem of a verb isn't long and green, though. The *stem* of a verb refers to what you get when you remove the ending *-en* from the German infinitive. The *stem vowel* refers to the vowel in this stem. In English, for example, when you conjugate the verb *run* (I run, you run, she runs) it retains the same stem vowel throughout the conjugation. What exactly is meant here by conjugation? *Conjugation* refers to the changes in the verb (with weak verbs, the changes occur in the endings) which keep the verb agreeing with the subject.

Was haben Sie gesagt?

Conjugation The changes of the verb that occur to indicate who or what is performing the action (or undergoing the state of being) of the verb and when the action (or state of being) of the verb is occurring: in the present, the past, or the future.

Verbs Express Action

No matter what you do, you need verbs to express action, motion, or states of being. In German, the most common way of grouping verbs is weak, strong, or mixed. When verbs are conjugated, a relatively predictable pattern of endings is attached to the stem of weak verbs. Strong verbs have a relatively predictable pattern of endings when they are conjugated in the present tense (the form a verb takes to indicate that action is occurring in the present), but both the stem and the endings become irregular (they don't follow a set pattern) in the past tense. Mixed verbs have features of both weak and strong verbs.

The rest of this chapter examines weak and strong verbs in the present tense. Mixed verbs are discussed in Chapter 7.

Was haben Sie gesagt?

Weak Verbs   Verbs that follow a set pattern of rules and retain the same stem vowel throughout their conjugation.

Some Verbs Are Weaker Than Others

In Chapter 3, you learned about the infinitive, or unconjugated, form of verbs. Weak verbs are verbs that, when conjugated, follow a set pattern of rules and retain the same stem vowel throughout. Think of them as being too "weak" to alter the patterns they follow. Let's follow *fly* through its full conjugation:

Person	Singular	Plural
First	I fly	we fly
Second	you fly	you fly
Third	he/she flies	they fly

The majority of German verbs fall into the category of weak verbs (see Table 5.1).

Table 5.1   Conjugation of a Weak Verb I: leben

Person	Singular	English	Plural	English
First	ich lebe *iH ley-buh*	I live	wir leben *veeR ley-buhn*	we live
Second	du lebst *dew leybst*	you live	ihr lebt *eeR leybt*	you live
Formal (sing. and plural)	Sie leben *zee ley-buhn*	you live		
Third	er, sie, es lebt *eR, zee, es lebt*	he, she, it lives	sie leben *zee ley-buhn*	they live

Verbs whose stem ends in *-d*, *-t*, *-n*, or *-tm* keep the *-e* after the stem throughout the conjugation (see Table 5.2).

Table 5.2   Conjugation of a Weak Verb II: reden

Person	Singular	English	Plural	English
First	ich rede *iH Rey-duh*	I talk	wir reden *veeR Rey-duhn*	we talk
Second	du redest *dew Rey-dest*	you talk	ihr redet *eeR Rey-duht*	you talk
Formal (sing. and plural)	Sie reden *zee Rey-duhn*	you talk		
Third	er, sie, es redet *eR, zee, es Rey-duht*	he, she, it talks	sie reden *zee Rey-duhn*	they talk

How Do You End a Weak Verb?

Think of weak verbs as timid, law-abiding creatures that would never cross the street when the light is red. This is the great thing (for those of you embarking on learning the German language) about weak verbs: they obey grammar laws and follow a predictable pattern of conjugation. Once you've learned this pattern (and the few exceptions to this pattern), you should be able to conjugate weak verbs in German without too much difficulty. To conjugate weak verbs, drop the *-en* from the infinitive and then add the following endings:

Person	Singular	Ending	Plural	Ending
First	ich	*e*	wir	*en*
Second	du	*(e)st*	ihr	*(e)t*
Formal (sing. and plural)	Sie	*en*		
Third	er, sie, es	*(e)t*	sie	*en*

Achtung!

There are a small number of verbs whose infinitives take *-n* and not *-en*. The conjugated form of these verbs in the first and third person plural is the same as the infinitive form. *Handeln* (*hAn-duhln*), which means "to act," becomes *wir/sie handeln* (we/they act) in the first and third person plural.

In Table 5.3 you will find some of the most commonly used weak verbs in German. Read through them a few times, and see if you can commit them to memory.

Some Verbs Are Strong

Verbs don't, of course, lift weights or have muscles. You can't tell the difference between a strong verb and a weak verb just by looking at them. The only way you can distinguish between them is to look up their conjugations and see whether the stem changes.

Table 5.3 Common Weak Verbs

Verb	Meaning	Pronunciation
antworten	*Ant-voR-tuhn*	to answer
arbeiten	*AR-bay-tuhn*	to work
blicken	*bli-kuhn*	to look, glance
brauchen	*bRou-CHuhn*	to need
danken	*dAn-kuhn*	to thank
fragen	*fRah-guhn*	to ask
glauben	*glou-buhn*	to believe
kosten	*ko-stuhn*	to cost, to taste, to try
lernen	*leR-nuhn*	to learn, to study
lieben	*lee-buhn*	to love
machen	*mA-CHuhn*	to make, to do
mieten	*mee-tuhn*	to rent
rauchen	*Rou-CHuhn*	to smoke
reisen	*ray-suhn*	to travel
reservieren	*rey-seR-vee-Ruhn*	to reserve
sagen	*sah-guhn*	to say, to tell
schicken	*shi-kuhn*	to send
sehen	*zey-huhn*	to see
spielen	*shpee-luhn*	to play
suchen	*zew-Huhn*	to look for
tanzen	*tAn-tsuhn*	to dance
telefonieren	*tey-ley-foh-nee-Ruhn*	to telephone
warten	*vAR-tuhn*	to wait
wohnen	*voh-nuhn*	to reside
zeigen	*tsay-guhn*	to show, to indicate

Was haben Sie gesagt?

Strong Verb A verb whose stem vowel undergoes a
change or a modification when conjugated in the past
tense. Only some strong verbs undergo a vowel modification in the present tense.

It's Not Easy Being Strong

Strong verbs are "strong" because they alter the patterns
that "weaker" verbs follow. Some strong verbs change
their stem vowel in the present tense; the endings, however, are the same for both weak and strong verbs in all
tenses. In the present tense, there are some changes that
occur in the second and third person in the stem vowel:

➤ *a, o, u* becomes *ä, ö, ü*

➤ *e* changes into *-i*, or *-ie*

➤ *au* changes into *äu*

Table 5.4 Conjugation of a Strong Verb I: sehen

Person	Singular	English	Plural	English
First	ich sehe *iH zey-huh*	I see	wir sehen *veeR zey-huhn*	we see
Second	du siehst *dew zeest*	you see	ihr seht *eeR zeyt*	you see
Formal (sing. and plural)	Sie sehen *zee zey-huhn*	you see		
Third	er, sie, es sieht *eR, zee, es zeet*	he, she, it sees	sie sehen *zee zey-huhn*	they see

Table 5.5   Conjugation of a Strong Verb II: fallen

Person	Singular	English	Plural	English
First	ich falle *iH fA-luh*	I fall	wir fallen *veeR fA-luhn*	we fall
Second	du fällst *dew fälst*	you fall	ihr fallt *eeR fAlt*	you fall
Formal	Sie fallen *zee fa-luhn*	you fall		
Third	er, sie, es fällt *eR, zee, es fält*	he, she, it falls	sie fallen *zee fA-luhn*	they fall

In Table 5.6, you will find some commonly used strong verbs. Read through them a few times, as you did with the weak verbs. You shouldn't have too much trouble memorizing them—many of them are near cognates!

Table 5.6   Common Strong Verbs

Verb	Pronunciation	Meaning
beginnen	*be-gi-nuhn*	to begin
bleiben	*blay-buhn*	to remain
essen	*es-uhn*	to eat
fahren	*fah-ruhn*	to drive
finden	*fin-duhn*	to find
fliegen	*flee-guhn*	to fly
geben	*gey-buhn*	to give
halten	*hAl-tuhn*	to hold/to stop
helfen	*hel-fuhn*	to help
leiden	*lay-duhn*	to suffer
lesen	*ley-zuhn*	to read
nehmen	*ney-muhn*	to take
schlafen	*shlah-fuhn*	to sleep

continues

Table 5.6 Continued

Verb	Pronunciation	Meaning
schreiben	*shray-buhn*	to write
sprechen	*shpRe-Huhn*	to speak
treffen	*tRe-fuhn*	to meet
trinken	*tRin-kuhn*	to drink

How Do You Show You're Asking a Question?

Okay, now go back to where you were at the beginning of this chapter, planning a trip. Suppose you're planning another trip—alone, this time. You'll probably find that there are a lot of questions you'll want to ask when you get where you're going. You'll deal with more complicated questions in Chapter 10. For now, stick to the easy questions—the ones that can be answered with a simple yes or no.

There are other ways, besides the confused look on your face, to show that you're asking a question: through intonation, the addition of the tag *nicht wahr*, and inversion.

Rising Your Inflection

One of the easiest ways to indicate you're asking a question is by simply raising your voice slightly at the end of the sentence. To do this, speak with a rising *inflection*.

Du denkst an die Reise?
Dew denkst An dee Ray-zuh
Are you thinking about the trip?

Sagen Sie mal...

One easy way of forming questions in German is by adding the tag *nicht wahr* (*niHt vahR*) to your statements. *Nicht wahr* means, "Isn't this true?"

Du denkst an die Reise, nicht wahr?
Dew denkst An dee Ray-zuh, niHt vahR
You think about the trip, don't you?

Turn It Upside Down

The final way of forming a question is by *inversion*. Inversion is what you do when you reverse the word order of the subject nouns or pronouns and the conjugated form of the verb. If you're up to the challenge of inversion, follow these rules:

➤ Avoid inverting with *ich*. It's awkward and rarely done.

➤ Only invert subject nouns or pronouns with conjugated verbs. Read the following examples and see if you can get a feel for how inversion works.

Du gehst nach Hause.	Gehst du nach Hause?
Er spricht Deutsch.	Spricht er Deutsch?
Wir reisen nach Berlin.	Reisen wir nach Berlin?
Ihr eβt Sauerkraut.	Eβt ihr Sauerkraut?
Sie trinken Bier.	Trinken sie Bier?
Du fährst mit dem Zug.	Fährst du mit dem Zug?

Remember that whether you are using intonation, nicht wahr, or inversion, you are asking for exactly the same information: a yes or no (*ja oder nein*) answer.

Now You've Got to Answer the Question

If you are someone who has learned to look on the bright side of things, you'll probably want to know how to answer "yes." To answer in the affirmative, use *ja* (*yah*), and then give your statement.

Sprichst du Deutsch?	Ja, ich spreche Deutsch.
shpRiHst doo doytsh	*yah, iH shpRe-Huh doytsh*

Or if your time is valuable and you are constantly being harangued to do things you have no interest in doing, you should probably learn to say "no." To answer negatively, use *nein* (*nayn*) at the beginning of the statement, and then add *nicht* (*niHt*) at the end of the statement.

Rauchen Sie?	Nein, ich rauche nicht.
Rou-Chuhn zee	*nayn, iH Rou-CHuh niHt*

You can vary the forms of your negative answers by putting the following negative phrases before and after the conjugated verb.

...nie(mals)	Never
nee(mahls)	
Ich rauche nie(mals).	I never smoke.
iH Rou-CHuh nee(mahls).	
...nicht mehr	No longer
niHt meyR	
Ich rauche nicht mehr.	I no longer smoke.
iH Rou-CHuh niHt meyR	
...(gar)nichts	Anything, nothing
(gAR)niHts	
Ich rauche nichts.	I'm not smoking anything.
iH Rou-CHuh niHts	

If you want to form simple sentences in the present tense, you'll need to have as many verbs as possible at the tip of your tongue. Review Tables 5.3 and 5.6, which provide you with lists of the most frequently used weak and strong verbs.

Chapter 6

Getting to Know You

In This Chapter

➤ Common greetings and introductions

➤ The verb *sein*

➤ How to ask for information

➤ Expressing possession

➤ The irregular verb *haben*

In the previous chapter, you learned how to create simple German sentences (using subject nouns, pronouns, and verbs) and how to ask basic yes or no questions. Now you're going to put some of what you learned to work. It's time to start engaging in conversation.

You are sitting alone on an airplane, admiring the view of clouds and sky through the window. The person in the seat next to you is German; it's time to use this opportunity to test some of your newly acquired language skills.

How Do You Do?

You may find the following conversation openers useful.

Sagen Sie mal...

Saying Hello "Hallo" is informal for "hello" practically everywhere, but in Southern Germany and Austria, "Grüß Gott (*gRüs got*)" is used formally instead of "Guten Tag (*gew-tuhn tAk*)."

Formal Helloes

It is sometimes considered rude to use the *du* form of address with someone who isn't a friend or relative. Because you don't know the person you're speaking to, it is definitely best to take the formal approach. It is worth noting, however, that younger generations are tending more and more to use the informal *du* form.

German	Pronunciation	Meaning
Guten Tag.	*gew-tuhn tahk*	Hello.
Guten Abend.	*gew-tuhn ah-bent*	Good evening.
mein Herr	*mayn heR*	Sir
meine Dame	*may-nuh dah-muh*	Miss, Mrs.
Ich heibe...	*iH hay-suh*	My name is...
Wie heiben Sie?	*vee hay-suhn zee*	What is your name?
Wie geht es Ihnen?	*vee gayt es ee-nuhn*	How are you?
Sehr gut.	*zeyR gewt*	Very well.

German	Pronunciation	Meaning
Nicht schlecht.	*niHt shleHt*	Not bad.
Es geht so.	*es gayt zo*	So so.

Informal Helloes

You hit it off with your plane buddy right away, and he says, "Dutzen Sie mich, bitte (*dew-tsuhn zee miH, bi-tuh*)," which means, "Please, use *du* with me." When this happens, it means that you've earned the right to a certain degree of intimacy with this person. You can now use the following phrases:

German	Pronunciation	Meaning
Hallo!	*hA-lo*	Hi!
Ich heibe...	*iH hay-suh*	My name is...
Wie heibt du?	*vee hayst dew*	What is your name?
Wie geht's?	*vee gayts*	How are you?
Wie geht es dir?	*vee gayt es deeR*	How's it going with you?
Was machst du so?	*vAs mACHst dew zo*	What's up?
Ganz gut.	*gAns gewt*	Okay.
Ich kann nicht klagen.	*iH kAn niHt klah-guhn*	I can't complain.
Mal so, mal so.	*Mahl zo, mahl zo.*	So so.

So Where Are You From?

Eventually, you are going to want to know where the person to whom you are speaking is from. You also are going to want to respond correctly when he asks you where you are from. To do this, you will need to familiarize yourself with the irregular verb *kommen* (*ko-muhn*) (see Table 6.1).

Table 6.1   The Verb kommen

Person	Singular	English	Plural	English
First	ich komme *iH ko-muh*	I come	wir kommen *veeR ko-muhn*	we come
Second	du kommst *dew komst*	you come	Sie kommen *zee ko-muhn*	you come
(Formal)	ihr kommt *eeR komt*		Sie kommen *zee ko-muhn*	
Third	er, sie, es kommt *eR, zee, es komt*	he, she, it comes	sie kommen *zee ko-muhn*	they come

To question someone about his or her origins, try the following:

Formal use:

> Woher kommen Sie?
> *voh-heR ko-muhn zee*
> Where are you from?

Informal use:

> Woher kommst du?   Ich komme aus…
> *voh-heR komst dew*   *itt ko-muh ous*
> Where are you from?   I come from…

Keep in mind that most countries, towns, and cities are neuter nouns and take the article *das*. *Die USA* (*dee ew-es-ah*) and *die Vereinigten Staaten* (*dee feR-ay-nik-tuhn shtah-tuhn*), or United States, are exceptions; because they are plural, they take the plural article *die*. Some other exceptions are: *die Schweiz* (*dee shvayts*), or Switzerland, *die Türkei* (*dee tüR-kay*), *der Irak* (*deyR ee-Rahk*), *der Iran* (*deyR ee-Rahn*), *der Libanon* (*deyR lee-bah-non*), or Lebanon, *der Kongo* (*deyR kon-go*), or Congo. When you use countries, cities, or towns with the neuter article, drop the article *das*:

Ich komme aus New York.
iH ko-muh ous new yoRk

Ich komme aus Amerika.
iH ko-muh ous ah-mey-Ree-kah

Be careful with countries that take *der* and *die* articles. The articles are not dropped, and they must be declined correctly (that is to say, they must take the appropriate case).

Die USA, which is plural, takes the dative plural article *den*:

Ich komme aus den USA.
iH ko-muh ous deyn ew-es-ah

Die Schweiz, which is feminine, takes the feminine dative article *der*:

Ich komme aus der Schweiz.
iH ko-muh ous deyR shvayts

Der Libanon, which is masculine, takes the masculine dative article *dem*:

Ich komme aus dem Libanon.
iH ko-muh ous deym lee-bah-non

Achtung!

It's generally considered quite rude to address someone informally unless you have established a friendship or bond with them. To *dutzen* (*dew-tsuhn*) someone—in other words, to use the informal *du* form of address with a person—may alienate the stranger, distant relative, or business acquaintance you are addressing. Generally, you have to earn the privilege to use the informal *du* with people you don't know.

Conjugating "To Be": Sein

After you've established where someone is from, you will probably want to find out more about what he does. But what if, instead of answering you directly, he gives you a whimsical smile, and says, "Raten Sie mal (*Rah-tuhn zee mahl*)," which means, bluntly, "Guess." What can you do? You'll probably have to recite a list of professions in the hopes that sooner or later you'll happen on the right one. To do this, you should learn the conjugation of the irregular verb *sein* (*zayn*), or "to be." See Table 6.2.

Table 6.2   The Verb sein

Person	Singular	English	Plural	English
First	ich bin *iH bin*	I am	wir sind *veeR zint*	we are
Second	du bist *dew bist*	you are	ihr seid *eeR zayt*	you are
(Formal)	Sie sind *zee zint*		Sie sind *zee zint*	
Third	er, sie, es ist *eR, zee, es ist*	he, she, it is	sie sind *zee zint*	they are

Formal:

> Was sind Sie von Beruf?
> *VAs sint zee fon bey-Rewf*
> What is your profession?

Informal:

> Was bist du von Beruf?
> *VAs bist dew fon bey-Rewf*
> What is your profession?

> Was machst du?
> *vAs maCHst dew*
> What do you do?

> Ich bin...
> *iH bin...*
> I am...

Sagen Sie mal...

In German, the indefinite article *ein(e)* is generally not used when a person states his profession unless the profession is qualified by an adjective. To say, "I'm a police officer," you would say, "Ich bin Polizist (*ich bin poh-lee-tsist*)." To say, "I'm a good police officer," however, you would say, "Ich bin ein guter Polizist (*iH bin ayn gew-tuhR poh-lee-tsist*)."

Table 6.3 Professions

Profession	Pronunciation	English
der Kellner (die Kellnerin)	*deyR kel-nuhR* (*dee kel-nuh-Rin*)	waiter, waitress
der Sekretär (die Sekretärin)	*deyR sek-Rey-tähR* (*dee sek-Rey-täh-Rin*)	secretary
der Arzt (die Ärztin)	*deyR ARtst* (*dee ÄRts-tin*)	doctor
der Doktor	*deyR dok-tohR*	doctor
der Elektriker (die Elektrikerin)	*deyR ey-lek-tRi-kuhR* (*dee ey-lek-tRi-kuh-Rin*)	electrician
der Student (die Studentin)	*deyR shtew-dent* (*dee shtew-den-tin*)	student
der Krankenpfleger (die Krankenschwester)	*deyR kRAn-kuhn-pfley-guhR* (*dee kRAn-kuhn-shves-tuhR*)	nurse
der Mechaniker (die Mechanikerin)	*deyR mey-Hah-ni-kuhR* (*die mey-Hah-ni-kuh-Rin*)	mechanic
der Feuerwehrmann	*deyR foy-uhR-veyR-mAn*	firefighter

continues

Table 6.3 Continued

Profession	Pronunciation	English
der Friseur (die Frieseuse)	*deyR fRee-zöhR* (*dee fRee-zöh-zuh*)	hairdresser
der Rechtsanwalt (die Rechtsanwältin)	*deyR ReHts-An-vAlt* (*dee ReHts-An-väl-tin*)	lawyer
der Polizist (die Polizistin)	*deyR poh-lee-tsist* (*dee poh-lee-tsis-tin*)	policeman, policewoman, police officer

Curiosity Killed the Cat—But You're Not a Cat

One of the advantages of learning a new language is that you can get away with acting a little childish. So get nosy. Start asking about everything. Make *faux pas*. People will think you're just trying to expand your vocabulary.

Table 6.4 Information Questions

German	Pronunciation	English
mit wem	*mit vem*	with whom
um wieviel Uhr	*oom vee-feel ooR*	at what time
von wem	*von vem*	of, about, from whom
wann	*vAn*	when
warum/wieso/ weshalb	*va-Rum/vee-soh/ ves-hAlp*	why
was	*vAs*	what
wer	*veR*	who
wie	*vee*	how
wieviel	*vee-feel*	how much, many
wo	*voh*	where
woher	*voh-heR*	from where

German	Pronunciation	English
wohin	*voh-hin*	where (to)
womit/ mit was	*voh-mit/ mit vas*	with what
worüber	*voh-Rüh-buhR*	what about
wovon/von was	*voh-fon/fon vas*	of, about, from what
zu wem	*tsoo vem*	to whom

Breaking the Ice

Here are some ways of breaking the ice.

Formal	Pronunciation	English
Mit wem reisen Sie? *mit vem Ray-zuhn zee*	Mit wem reist du? *mit vem Rayst dew*	With whom are you traveling?
Warum reisen Sie? *vah-Room Ray-zuhn zee*	Warum reist du? *vah-Room Rayst dew*	Why are you traveling?
Wie lange reisen Sie? *vee lAn-guh Ray-zuhn zee*	Wie lange reist du? *vee lAn-guh Rayst dew*	For how long are you traveling?
Wo wohnen Sie? *voh voh-nuhn zee*	Wo wohnst du? *voh vohnst dew*	Where do you live?

It's a Family Affair

Have you ever been introduced to a group of people sitting around a table and said, "Oh, and this must be your lovely daughter," only to find yourself the object of puzzled, nervous glances? Was the silence broken when the gentleman you were addressing said, "Actually, no. This is my wife." Of course, if you find yourself putting your foot in your mouth in German, you can always claim that you are still learning your vocabulary. Start practicing now with the following words for family members in Table 6.5.

Table 6.5   Family Members

Male	Pronunciation	English
das Kind	*dAs kint*	child
der (Ehe) Mann	*deyR (ey-huh)mAn*	husband
der Bruder	*deyR brew-duhR*	brother
der Cousin	*deyR kew-zahN*	cousin
der Opa/Grobvater	*deyR oh-pah/gRohs-fah-tuhR*	grandfather
der Schwiegersohn	*deyR shvee-guhR-zohn*	son-in-law
der Vater	*deyR fah-tuhR*	father

Female	Pronunciation	English
das Kind	*dAs kint*	child
die (Ehe) Frau	*dee (ey-huh)fRou*	wife
die Schwester	*dee shves-tuhR*	sister
die Cousine	*die kew-see-nuh*	cousin
die Oma/Grobmutter	*dee oh-mah/gRohs-moo-tuhR*	grandmother
die Schwiegertochter	*dee shvee-guhR-toCH-tuhR*	daughter-in-law
die Mutter	*dee moo-tuhR*	mother

Here are some useful plurals and their spellings:

Plural	Pronunciation	English
die Kinder	*dee kin-duhR*	the children
die Eltern	*dee el-tuhRn*	the parents
die Grobeltern	*dee gRohs-el-tuhRn*	the grandparents
die Schweigereltern	*dee shvee-guhR-el-tuhRn*	the in-laws

We're All Somebody's Something: Possession and the Genitive Case

We're all somebody's something. You're your mother's daughter or son, your uncle's nephew or niece, your wife's husband or your husband's wife. There are two principal ways of showing possession in German: by using the genitive case and by using possessive adjectives.

The genitive case is used to show possession or dependence. To do this, you must decline the noun and the noun marker correctly. Have you forgotten what noun marker means? Refresh your memory: Noun marker refers to any of a variety of articles, such as *der*, *die*, *das*, or *die* (the equivalent of "the" for plural nouns), *ein* (the equivalent of "a" for masculine or neuter nouns), or *eine* (the equivalent of "a" for feminine nouns). See Chapter 4 for how to decline masculine, feminine, and neuter nouns in the genitive case. Here is an abbreviated version of the declension of the definite articles *der, die,* and *das* and of the plural article *die*. When you use proper names or are speaking of family members possessing someone or something, you can use the genitive *-s* to show possession (add the *-s* without an apostrophe to the end of the word).

Masc.	Fem.	Neuter	Plural (All Genders)
des	der	des	der

German	Pronunciation	Meaning
Das ist der Sohn des Mannes.	*dAs ist deyR zohn des mA-nuhs*	That is the man's son.
Das ist der Ehemann der Frau.	*dAs ist deyR ey-huh-mAn deyR fRou*	That is the woman's husband.
Die Mutter des Kindes ist schön.	*dee moo-tuhR des kin-duhs ist shöhn.*	The child's mother is beautiful.

Was haben Sie gesagt?

Genitive –s This method of showing possession can be used with family members and proper names. To say, "Stephanie's father," you would say, *Stephanies Vater* (*ste-fah-nees fah-tuhR*). To say, "father's daughter," you would say, *Vaters Tochter* (*fah-tuhRs toH-tuhR*).

Possessive Adjectives The adjectives mein, dein, sein, ihr, and unser show that something belongs to someone.

You Are What You Own

The possessive adjectives my, your, his, her, and so on, show that something belongs to somebody. In German, possessive adjectives agree in number and gender with the noun they are describing (that is to say, with the thing being possessed rather than with the possessor). Keep in mind that in the singular, the endings for possessive adjectives are the same ones used for the declension of the indefinite article *ein*.

English	German
He loves his father.	Er liebt seinen Vater. *eyR leept zay-nuhn fah-tuhR.*
He loves his mother.	Er liebt seine Mutter. *eyR leept zay-nuh moo-tuhR*
She loves her father.	Sie liebt ihren Vater. *Zee leept ee-Ruhn fah-tuhR*
She loves her mother.	Sie liebt ihre Mutter. *zee leept ee-Ruh moo-tuhR*

Table 6.6 shows you the possessive adjectives and Tables 6.7 and 6.8 help you with the declension of these adjectives.

Table 6.6   Possessive Adjectives

Person	Singular	Meaning	Plural	Meaning
First	mein *mayn*	my	unser *oon-zuhR*	our
Second	dein *dayn*	your	euer *oy-uhR*	your
(Formal)	Ihr *eeR*		Ihr *eeR*	
Third	sein, ihr, sein *zayn, eeR, zayn*	his, her, its	ihr *eeR*	their

Table 6.7   The Declension of the Possessive Adjective I

Case	Masculine "your man "	Feminine "your woman"	Neuter "your child"
Nom.	dein Mann *dayn mAn*	deine Frau *day-nuh fRou*	dein Kind *dayn kint*
Acc.	deinen Mann *day-nuhn mAn*	deine Frau *day-nuh fRou*	dein Kind *dayn kint*
Dat.	deinem Mann *day-nuhm mAn*	deiner Frau *day-nuhR fRou*	deinem Kind *day-nuhm kint*
Gen.	deines Mann(e)s *day-nuhs mAn(uh)s*	deiner Frau *day-nuhR fRou*	deines Kind(e)s *day-nuhs kind(uh)s*

Table 6.8 The Declension of the Possessive Adjective II

Case	Masculine "your man"	Feminine "your woman"	Neuter "your child"
Nom.	deine Männer *day-nuh mä-nuhR*	deine Frauen *day-nuh fRou-uhn*	deine Kinder *day-nuh kin-duhR*
Acc.	deine Männer *day-nuh mä-nuhR*	deine Frauen *day-nuh fRou-uhn*	deine Kinder *day-nuh kin-duhR*
Dat.	deinen Männern *day-nuhn mä-nuhR*	deinen Frauen *day-nuhn fRou-uhn*	deinen Kindern *day-nuhn kin-duhR*
Gen.	deiner Männer *day-nuhR mä-nuhR*	deiner Frauen *day-nuhR fRou-uhn*	deiner Kinder *day-nuhR kin-duhR*

Achtung!

There are many meanings in German for the word *ihr* (*eeR*). As a possessive adjective it can mean *her, their,* or *your*. One way of avoiding confusion in written German is by remembering to capitalize *Ihr* when it means *your*.

Memorizing the Verb Haben

A verb that you will find useful when you have a conversation with someone is the verb *haben* (*hah-buhn*), to have. In German, you use this verb to express many things concerning yourself, including how long you've been living in a particular place. Like the verbs *kommen* and *sein, haben* is irregular and there's just no way around it: You've got to bite the bullet and memorize its conjugation.

Table 6.9 The Verb haben

Person	Singular	Meaning	Plural	Meaning
First	ich habe *iH hah-buh*	I have	wir haben *veeR hah-buhn*	we have
Second	du hast *dew hAst*	you have	ihr habt *eeR hAbt*	you have
(Formal)	Sie haben *zee hah-buhn*		Sie haben *zee hah-buhn*	
Third	er, sie, es, hat *eyR, zee, es, hAt*	he, she, it, has	sie haben *zee hah-buhn*	they have

Adjectives Describe, But Don't Always Decline

If you want to describe someone or something, you will need to use descriptive adjectives. German adjectives decline—when they come immediately before the noun, they agree in gender (masculine, feminine, or neuter), number (singular or plural), and case (nominative, accusative, dative, or genitive). Many adjectives, however, don't precede a noun or form a part of the noun. These adjectives—ones that occur after the noun—don't decline.

A declining adjective:

Die kranke Frau schläft.
dee kRAn-kuh fRou shläft
The sick woman sleeps.

A non-declining adjective:

Die Frau ist krank.
dee fRou ist kRAnk
The woman is sick.

Declining Adjectives: A Matter of Strength

Adjectives can have weak, strong, or mixed declensions. Weak adjective endings are used after a word that *already shows gender and case*. Because the adjective ending doesn't have to perform this function, it is "weak." If there is no word before the adjective showing gender and case, then the adjective has to do it and the ending must be "strong." Mixed declensions share characteristics of both weak and strong declensions. The good news is that these declensions are all quite regular.

The weak declension of adjectives is used after these words: *der* (the), *dieser* (this), *jeder* (each), *jener* (that), *mancher* (many a), *solcher* (such), *welcher* (which, what). See Table 6.10.

Table 6.10 The Weak Declension of an Adjective with a Singular Noun

Case	Masculine "the little boy"	Feminine "the little cat"	Neuter "the little pig"
Nom.	der kleine Junge *deyR klay-nuh* *yoon-guh*	die kleine Katze *dee klay-nuh* *kA-tzuh*	das kleine Schwein *dAs klay-nuh shvayn*
Acc.	den kleinen Jungen *deyn klay-nuhn* *yoon-guhn*	die kleine Katze *dee klay-nuh* *kA-tzuh*	das kleine Schwein *dAs klay-nuh shvayn*
Dat.	dem kleinen Jungen *deym klay-nuhn* *yoon-guhn*	der kleinen Katze *deyR klay-nuhn* *kA-tzuh*	dem kleinen Schwein *deym klay-nuhn* *shvayn*
Gen.	des kleinen Jungen *des klay-nuhn* *yoon-guhn*	der kleinen Katze *deyR klay-nuhn* *kA-tzuh*	des kleinen Schweins *des klay-nuhn shvayns*

Was haben Sie gesagt?

All adjectives, no matter how many there are, that precede a noun have the same ending: *das schöne, lustige, kleine, intelligente Mädchen* (the pretty, funny, small, intelligent girl).

As you can see in Table 6.11, adjectives with plural nouns in the weak declension all take the same ending: *-en*.

Table 6.11   The Weak Declension of an Adjective with a Plural Noun

Case	Masculine "the little boys"	Feminine "the little cats"	Neuter "the little pigs"
Nom.	die kleinen Jungen *dee klay-nuhn yoon-guhn*	die kleinen Katzen *dee klay-nuhn kA-tsuhn*	die kleinen Schweine *dee klay-nuhn shvay-nuh*
Acc.	die kleinen Jungen *dee klay-nuhn yoon-guhn*	die kleinen Katzen *dee klay-nuhn kA-tsuhn*	die kleinen Schweine *dee klay-nuhn shvay-nuh*
Dat.	den kleinen Jungen *deyn klay-nuhn yoon-guhn*	den kleinen Katzen *deyn klay-nuhn kA-tsuhn*	den kleinen Schweinen *deyn klay-nuhn shvay-nuh*
Gen.	der kleinen Jungen *deyR klay-nuhn yoon-guhn*	der kleinen Katzen *deyR klay-nuhn kA-tsuhn*	der kleinen Schweine *deyR klay-nuhn shvay-nuh*

When there is no article preceding a noun, adjectives take the strong declension: *Schönes Wetter, was?* (*shö-nuhs ve-tuhR, vAs*) Nice weather, isn't it? The strong declension is used after cardinal numbers:

drei weiße Blumen
dRay vay-suh blew-muhn
three white flowers

The strong declension also is used in the salutation of a letter:

Lieber Vater
lee-buhR fah-tuhR
Dear father

Table 6.12 The Strong Declension of an Adjective with a Singular Noun

Case	Masculine "beautiful moon"	Feminine "beautiful sun"	Neuter "beautiful girl"
Nom.	schöner Mond *shö-nuhR mohnt*	schöne Sonne *shöh-nuh zo-nuh*	schönes Mädchen *shöh-nuhs mät Huhn*
Acc.	schönen Mond *shö-nuhn mohnt*	schöne Sonne *shöh-nuh zo-nuh*	schönes Mädchen *shöh-nuhs mät Huhn*
Dat.	schönem Mond *shö-nuhm mohnt*	schöner Sonne *shöh-nuhR zo-nuh*	schönem Mädchen *shöh-nuhm mät-Huhn*
Gen.	schönen Monds *shö-nuhn mohnt*	schöner Sonne *shöh-nuhR zo-nuh*	schönen Mädchens *shöh-nuhn mät-Huhns*

Strong adjectives with masculine, feminine, and neuter plural nouns share the same declension. See Table 6.13.

Table 6.13 The Strong Declension of an Adjective with a Plural Noun

Case	Masculine "beautiful moons"	Feminine "beautiful suns"	Neuter "beautiful girls"
Nom.	schöne Monde *shö-nuh mohn-duh*	schöne Sonnen *shöh-nuh zo-nuhn*	schöne Mädchen *shöh-nuh mät-Huhn*
Acc.	schöne Monde *shö-nuh mohn-duh*	schöne Sonnen *shöh-nuh zo-nuhn*	schöne Mädchen *shöh-nuh mät-Huhn*
Dat.	schönen Monden *shö-nuhn mohn-duhn*	schönen Sonnen *shöh-nuhn zo-nuhn*	schönen Mädchen *shöh-nuhn mät-Huhn*
Gen.	schöner Monde *shö-nuhR mohn-duh*	schöner Sonnen *shöh-nuhR zo-nuhn*	schöner Mädchen *shöh-nuhR mät Huhn*

When adjectives come after the following words, they take the mixed declension: *ein, kein, mein, dein, sein, ihr,* (fem.) *unser, euer, ihr* (plural), *Ihr* (formal). See Table 6.14.

Table 6.14   The Mixed Declension of an Adjective with a Singular Noun

Case	Masculine "my big brother"	Feminine "my big sister"	Neuter "my big home "
Nom.	mein grober Bruder *mayn gRoh-suhR bRew-duhR*	meine grobe Schwester *may-nuh gRoh-suh shve-stuhR*	mein grobes Haus *mayn gRoh-suhs hous*
Acc.	meinen groben Bruder *may-nuhn gRoh-suhn bRew-duhR*	meine grobe Schwester *may-nuh gRoh-suh shve-stuhR*	mein grobes Haus *mayn gRoh-suhs hous*
Dat.	meinem groben Bruder *mayn-uhm gRoh-suhn bRew-duhR*	meiner groben Schwester *may-nuhR gRoh-suhn shve-stuhR*	meinem groben Haus *may-nuhm gRoh-suhn hous*
Gen.	meines groben Bruders *may-nuhs gRoh-suhR bRew-duhRs*	meiner groben Schwester *may-nuhR gRoh-suhn shve-stuhR*	meines groben Hauses *may-nuhs gRoh suhn hou-suhs*

The mixed declension of adjectives with plural nouns is the same as the weak declension of adjectives with plural nouns: All adjectives take the ending *-en*. See Table 6.15.

Table 6.15   The Mixed Declension of an Adjective with a Plural Noun

Case	Masculine	Feminine	Neuter
Nom.	meine groben Brüder *may-nuh gRoh-suhn bRüh-duhR*	meine groben Schwestern *may-nuh gRoh-suhn shve-stuhRn*	meine groβen Häuser *may-nuh gRoh-suhn hoy-suhR*
Acc.	meine groben Brüder *may-nuh gRoh-suhn bRüh-duhR*	meine groben Schwestern *may-nuh gRoh-suhn shve-stuhRn*	meine groβen Häuser *may-nuh gRoh-suhn hoy-suhR*

continues

Table 6.15 Continued

Case	Masculine	Feminine	Neuter
Dat.	meinen groben Brüdern *may-nuhn gRoh-suhn bRüh-duhRn*	meinen groben Schwestern *may-nuhn gRoh-suhn shve-stuhRn*	meinen großen Häusern *may-nuhn gRoh-suhn hoy-suhRn*
Gen.	meiner groben Brüder *may-nuhR gRoh-suhn bRüh-duhR*	meiner groben Schwestern *may-nuhR gRoh-suhn shve-stuhRn*	meiner großen Häuser *may-nuhR gRoh-suhn hoy-suhR*

Okay, let's get ready to go places!

Chapter 7

Getting Around

In This Chapter

➤ Transportation and hotels

➤ Directions, plus the verb *gehen*

➤ Getting help when you don't understand

➤ Time and numbers

➤ Mixed verbs and verbs with prefixes

This section gives you the vocabulary you need to get from the plane to the hotel.

Table 7.1   Inside the Plane

English	German	Pronunciation
(no) smoking	(nicht) Raucher	*(niHt) Rou-CHuhR*
airline	die Fluglinie	*dee flook-lee-nee-uh*
airplane	das Flugzeug	*dAs flook-tsoyk*

continues

Table 7.1 Continued

English	German	Pronunciation
airport	der Flughafen	*deyR flook-hah-fuhn*
by the window	am Fenster	*Am fen-stuhR*
emergency exit	der Notausgang	*deyR noht-ous-gAng*
gate	der Flugsteig	*deyR flook-tsoyk*
on the aisle	im Gang	*im gAng*
passenger	der Passagier	*deyR pA-sA-jeeR*
seat	der Sitz	*deyR zits*
takeoff	der Abflug	*deyR ap-flook*
terminal	der Terminal	*deyR teR-mee-nahl*

We've All Got Baggage: Inside the Airport

Table 7.2 gives you all the vocabulary you'll need to identify where you need to go in and around the airport.

Table 7.2 Inside the Airport

English	German	Pronunciation
arrival	die Ankunft	*dee An-koonft*
arrival time	die Ankunftszeit	*dee An-koonfts-tsayt*
baggage claim	die Gepackausgabe	*dee guh-pak-ous-gah-buh*
bus stop	die Bushaltestelle	*dee boos-hAl-tuh-shte-luh*
car rental	der Autoverleih	*deyR ou-toh-feR-lay*
carry-on luggage	das Handgepack	*dAs hAnt-guh-pak*
departure time	die Abflugzeit	*dee Ap-flook-tsayt*
destination	das Flugziel	*dAs flook-tseel*
elevators	der Aufzug	*deyR ouf-tsook*
exit	der Ausgang	*deyR ous-gAng*

English	German	Pronunciation
flight number	die Flugnummer	*dee flook-noo-muhR*
gate	der Flugsteig	*deyR flook-shtayk*
luggage cart	der Gepackwagen	*deyR guh-pak-vah-guhn*
money exchange office	die Geldwechselstube	*dee gelt-vek-suhl-shtew-buh*
passport control	die Paßkontrolle	*dee pAs-kon-tRo-luh*
security check	die Sicherheitskontrolle	*dee zi-HuhR-Hayts-kon-tRo-luh*
suitcase	der Koffer	*deyR ko-fuhR*
the airline company	die Fluggesellschaft	*dee flook-guh-zel-shAft*

Whither Thou Goest

You will undoubtedly find the verb *gehen* (to go) handy as you make your way out of the airport to the taxi stand. The sooner you commit the conjugation of the verb *gehen* (see Table 7.3) to memory, the sooner you'll get to wherever it is you're going.

Table 7.3 The Verb gehen

Person	Singular	English	Plural	English
First	ich gehe *iH gey-huh*	I go	wir gehen *veeR gey-huhn*	we go
Second	du gehst *dew geyst*	you go	sie gehen *zee gey-huhn*	you go
(Formal)	ihr geht *eeR geyt*		Sie gehen *zee gey-huhn*	
Third	er, sie, es geht *eR, zee, es geyt*	he, she, it goes	sie gehen *zee gey-huhn*	they go

Contraction with Gehen

The verb *gehen* is often followed by the preposition *zu* (to). When this preposition is used to indicate location, the entire prepositional phrase is dative, and if the location toward which the subject is heading is masculine (*der*) or neuter (*das*), *zu* contracts with the article *dem* to become *zum* (to the). A *contraction* is a single word made out of two words, as in the word "it's." In German, contractions don't take an apostrophe. When *gehen* is followed by the prepositions *auf* or *in*, the prepositional phrase is in the accusative; if the location toward which the subject is heading is neuter, *auf* contracts with *das* to become *aufs* and *in* contracts with *das* to become *ins*.

> Ich gehe zum Bahnhof.
> *iH gey-huh tsoom bahn-hohf*
> I'm going to the airport.

> Ich gehe zum Geschaft.
> *iH gey-huh tsoom guh-shaft*
> I'm going to the store.

If the location toward which the subject is heading is feminine, *zu* (to) contracts with the feminine dative article *der* (the) to become *zur* (to the).

> Ich gehe zur Kirche.
> *iH gey-huh tsooR keeR-Hu*
> I'm going to the church.

If the location toward which the subject is heading is neuter and the preposition being use is *in* or *auf* (to), *in* contracts with the neuter accusative article *das* (the) to become *ins* (to the). *Auf* contracts with the neuter accusative article *das* to become *aufs*.

> Ich gehe ins Kino.
> *ich gey-huh ins kee-noh*
> I go to the movies.

Er geht aufs Polizeirevier.
eR geyt oufs po-lee-zay-Ruh-veeR
He goes to the police station.

Was haben Sie gesagt?

Contraction A single word made out of two words. In German, no apostrophe is used.

Wo Ist?

What if the place you're looking for isn't within pointing distance? If this turns out to be the case, you'd better know the verbs people use when they give directions (see Table 7.4).

Table 7.4 Verbs Used When Giving Directions

German	Pronunciation	English
abbiegen*	*ap-bee-guhn*	to turn
gehen	*gey-huhn*	to go
laufen	*lou-fuhn*	to walk
nehmen	*ney-muhn*	to take
weitergehen*	*vay-tuhR-gey-huhn*	to go on, continue

Sagen Sie mal...

In certain situations, you use the preposition *nach* to
indicate where you are going.

With continents, countries and towns:

Ich gehe nach Berlin.
iH gey-huh nAH beR-lin
I'm going to Berlin.

When speaking of a direction; north, south, east, west:

Du gehst nach Norden.
dew geyst nAH noR-duhn
You're going north.

With prepositions that show direction:

Er geht nach rechts.
eR geyt nAH reHts
He's going to the right.

Some Verbs Are Separated from Their Prefixes

Some of the verbs in Table 7.4 (the ones with asterisks
next to them) have *separable prefixes*, verbal complements
that are placed at the end of the sentence when the verb is
conjugated (separable prefixes will be addressed at greater
length later in this chapter). Some of the most common
separable prefixes are *auf, hinuber, aus, an, hinunter, hinauf,
weiter, bei, mit, nach,* and *zu.* When you use a verb with
separable prefixes, the verb comes near the beginning of
the sentence and the prefix comes at the end:

Du biegst rechts ab.
dew beekst reHts Ap
You turn right.

Er geht weiter zum Terminal.
eyR geyt vay-tuhR tsoom teR-mee-nahl
He continues to the terminal.

Was haben Sie gesagt?

Prefix In German, a prefix is a word form that modifies the meaning of the basic word.

Separable Prefix Verbal complements that are placed at the end of the sentence when the verb is conjugated.

And Don't Forget Those Prepositions

Prepositions are useful for giving and receiving directions. *Prepositions* show the relationship of a noun to another word in a sentence. Table 7.5 contains some useful prepositions for getting where you want to go.

Table 7.5 Prepositions

German	Pronunciation	English
auf	*ouf*	on
bei	*bay*	at
fern	*feRn*	far
gegen	*gey-guhn*	against
hinter	*hin-tuhR*	behind

continues

Table 7.5 Continued

German	Pronunciation	English
in	*in*	in
nach	*naCH*	after
nah	*nah*	near
neben	*ney-buhn*	next to
ohne	*oh-nuh*	without
um...zu	*oom...tsew*	in order to
unter	*oon-tuhR*	under
von	*fon*	from
vor	*foR*	in front of
zu, nach	*tsew, naCH*	to, at
zwischen	*tsvi-shuhn*	between

Was haben Sie gesagt?

Prepositions Words that show the relation of a noun to another word in a sentence.

Are You Still Confused?

In addition to scratching your head like crazy, use some of the phrases in Table 7.6 to let people know that you just don't understand.

Table 7.6   Expressing Incomprehension and Confusion

German	Pronunciation	English
Entschuldigen Sie	*ent-shool-dee-guhn zee*	Excuse me (formal)
Entschuldigung, ich habe Sie nicht verstanden	*ent-shool-dee-goonk, iH hah-buh zee niHt feR-shtan-duhn*	Excuse me, I didn't understand you.
Ich verstehe nicht.	*iH feR-shtey-huh niHt*	I don't understand.
Sprechen Sie langsamer, bitte.	*shpRe-Hun zee lAng-zah-muhR, bi-tuh*	Please speak more slowly.
Was haben Sie gesagt?	*vAs hah-buhn zee guh-zahkt*	What did you say?
Wiederholen Sie, bitte.	*vee-deR-hoh-luhn zee, bi-tuh*	Please repeat (what you just said).

Ground Transportation

Whether you see yourself zipping along on the Autobahn with a WWI flying-ace scarf trailing behind you, or hob-nobbing with the locals on a bus, knowing the words listed here will help you get around.

German	Pronunciation	English
das Auto	*dAs ou-toh*	car
das Taxi	*dAs tAk-see*	taxi
der Bus	*deyR boos*	bus
der Zug	*deyR tsewk*	train
die U-Bahn, S-Bahn	*dee ew-bahn, es-bahn*	subway
die Strabenbahn	*dee shtRah-suhn-bahn*	streetcar

Taking Advantage of *Nehmen*

You'll use the verb *nehmen* (*ney-muhn*), to take, to express how you are going to get from where you are to where you are going. *Nehmen* can be classified as a strong verb. The stem vowel e changes to i and the silent h is dropped in the second and third person singular forms (see Table 7.7).

Table 7.7   The Verb nehmen

Person	Singular	English	Plural	English
First	ich nehme *iH ney-muh*	I take	wir nehmen *veeR ney-muhn*	we take
Second	du nimmst *dew nimmst*	you take	ihr nehmt *eeR neymt*	you take
(Formal)	Sie nehmen *zee ney-muhn*			
Third	er, sie, es nimmt *eR, zee, es nimt*	he, she, it takes	sie nehmen *zee ney-muhn*	they take

Which Is the Most Indispensable German Word?

When you're traveling—and particularly when you're asking directions—one word in German will be indispensable to you: *welcher* (*vel-HuhR*), the word for "which" or "what." When *welcher* comes immediately before a noun and introduces a question, it is considered an interrogative pronoun and must agree in number, gender, and case with the noun it precedes. Some common pronouns that follow the same declension patterns as *welcher* are: *dieser* (this), *jeder* (each, every), *mancher* (many, many a), and *solcher* (such, such a). Tables 7.8 and 7.9 give the declension of *welcher* with singular and plural nouns.

Table 7.8   The Pronoun Welcher with Singular Nouns

Case	Masculine "which bus"	Feminine "which direction"	Neuter "which car"
Nom.	welcher Bus *vel-HuhR boos*	welche Richtung *vel-Huh RiH-toong*	welches Auto *vel-Huhs ou-toh*
Acc.	welchen Bus *vel-Huhn boos*	welche Richtung *vel-Huh RiH-toong*	welches Auto *vel-Huhs ou-toh*
Dat.	welchem Bus *vel-Huhm boos*	welcher Richtung *vel-HuhR RiH-toong*	welchem Auto *vel-Huhm ou-toh*
Gen.	welches Buses *vel-Huhs boosuhs*	welcher Richtung *vel-HuhR RiH-toong*	welches Autos *vel-Huhs ou-toh*

Table 7.9   The Pronoun Welcher with Plural Nouns

Case	Masculine "which buses"	Feminine "which directions"	Neuter "which cars"
Nom.	welche Buse *vel-Huh boo-suh*	welche Richtungen *vel-Huh RiH-toon-guhn*	welche Autos *vel-Huh ou-tohs*
Acc.	welche Buse *vel-Huh boo-suh*	welche Richtungen *vel-Huh RiH-toon-guhn*	welche Autos *vel-Huh ou-tohs*
Dat.	welchen Busen *vel-Huhn boo-suhn*	welchen Richtungen *vel-Huhn RiH-toon-guhn*	welchen Autos *vel-Huhn ou-tohs*
Gen.	welcher Buse *vel-HuhR boo-suh*	welcher Richtungen *vel-HuhR RiH-toon-guhn*	welcher Autos *vel-HuhR ou-tohs*

Renting a Car

You may want to take a trip around the countryside and the ideal way to do that is to rent a car. The following phrases are useful when renting a car.

Ich mochte ein Auto mieten.
iH moH-tuh ayn ou-toh mee-tuhn
I would like to rent a car.

Wieviel kostet es am Tag (in der Woche)?
vee-feel kos-tuht es Am tahk (in deyR vo-CHuh)
How much does it cost per day (per week)?

Welches Auto empfehlen Sie mir?
vel-Huhs ou-toh em-pfey-luhn zee meeR
Which car do you recommend?

Ist das Benzin im Preis enthalten?
ist dAs ben-tseen im pRays ent-hAl-tuhn
Is the gasoline included in the price?

Wie teuer ist die Versicherung?
vee toy-uhR ist dee veR-si-Huh-Roong
How expensive is the insurance?

If you decide to rent a car, don't forget to check in the trunk for the regulation jack—in German, *der Wagenheber* (*deyR vah-guhn-hey-buhR*)—and the spare tire, or *der Ersatzreifen* (*deyR eR-zAts-Ray-fuhn*). It also might be helpful you if you can ask someone if you're heading in the right direction. You never know when you're going to get lost in the woods without your compass.

nach Norden
nahCH noR-duhn
to the north

nach Suden
nahCH suh-duhn
to the south

nach Westen
nahCH ves-tuhn
to the west

nach Osten
nahCH os-tuhn
to the east

Eins, Zwei, Drei...

One, two, three, four ... as children, one of the first things we learn to do is count (today's children, tomorrow's tax-payers). Numbers that express amounts are known as *cardinal numbers*. The sooner you learn cardinal numbers in German the better, because you're going to need to use numbers for everything from renting a car to locating your gate in an airport (see Table 7.10).

Was haben Sie gesagt?

Cardinal Numbers Numbers used in counting.

Table 7.10   Cardinal Numbers

German	Pronunciation	English
null	*nool*	0
eins	*aynts*	1
zwei	*tsvay*	2
drei	*dRay*	3
vier	*feeR*	4
fünf	*fünf*	5
sechs	*zeks*	6
sieben	*zee-buhn*	7
acht	*aCHt*	8
neun	*noyn*	9
zehn	*tseyn*	10
elf	*elf*	11
zwülf	*tsvülf*	12
dreizehn	*dRay-tseyn*	13
vierzehn	*feeR-tseyn*	14…
zwanzig	*tsvAn-tsik*	20
einundzwanzig	*ayn-oont-tsvAn-tsik*	21
dreißig	*dRay-sik*	30
vierzig	*feeR-tsik*	40…

continues

Table 7.10 Continued

German	Pronunciation	English
hundert	*hoon-deRt*	100
hunderteins	*hoon-deRt-aynts*	101
zweihundert	*tsvay-hoon-deRt*	200 ...
tausend	*tou-zent*	1000
zweitausend	*tsvay-tou-zent*	2000 ...
hunderttausend	*hoon-deRt-tou-zent*	100,000 ...
eine Million	*aynuh mee-leeohn*	1,000,000
zwei Millionen	*tsvay mee-leeoh-nuhn*	2,000,000 ...
eine Milliarden	*ayn mee-lee-AR-duh*	1,000,000,000

Sagen Sie mal...

Because the sound of *zwei* (*tsvay*) and *drei* (*dRay*) is so similar, *zwo* (*tsvoh*) is often used for "two" in official language and when giving numbers on the telephone.

Timely Matters

Now that you have familiarized yourself with German numbers, it should be relatively easy for you to tell time. The simplest way to question someone about the time is by saying:

Wieviel Uhr ist es?   Wie spät ist es?
vee-feel ewR ist es   *vee shpäht ist es*
What time is it?   What time is it?

To answer a question about time, start out with *Es ist...* as in the examples that follow:

> Es ist...
> *es ist*
> It is...

Look at Table 7.11 for some common phrases to help you tell time.

Table 7.11   Telling Time

German	Pronunciation	English
Es ist ein Uhr.	*es ist ayn ewR*	It is 1:00.
Es ist fünf (Minuten) nach zwei.	*es ist fünf (mee-new-tuhn) nACH tsvay*	It is 2:05.
Es ist zehn nach halb acht.	*es ist tsehn nACH hAlp ACHt*	It is 8:40.
Es ist zwanzig vor neun.	*es ist tsvAn-tsik foR noyn*	It is 8:40.
Es ist Mitternacht.	*es ist mi-tuhR-nACHt*	It is midnight.
Es ist Mittag.	*es ist mi-tahk*	It is noon.

Now That You've Found Your Hotel

Before you hand over your credit card or traveler's check, be sure to verify with the people at *die Hotel Rezeption* (*dee hoh-tel Rey-tsep-tseeohn*) whether they can provide you with whatever it is you need: a quiet room, a wake-up call, or coffee at four a.m. Table 7.12 will help you get the scoop on just about everything a hotel has to offer.

Table 7.12   At the Hotel

German	Pronunciation	English
das Einkaufszentrum	*dAs ayn-koufs-tsen-tRoom*	shopping center
das Fitneßcenter	*dAs fit-nes-sen-tuhR*	fitness center

continues

Table 7.12 Continued

German	Pronunciation	English
das Geschäftszentrum	*dAs guh-shäfts-tsen-tRoom*	business center
der Geschenkladen	*deyR guh-shenk-lah-duhn*	gift shop
das Schwimmbad	*dAs shvim-baht*	swimming pool
das Zimmermädchen	*dAs tsi-muhR-mät-Huhn*	maid service
der (Gepäck)Träger	*deyR (guh-päk)tRäh-guhR*	porter
der Kassierer	*deyR kA-see-RuhR*	cashier
der Pförtner	*deyR pföRt-nuhR*	concierge
der Portier	*deyR poR-ti-ey*	doorman
der Zimmerservice	*deyR tsi-muhR-soR-vis*	room service
die Reinigung	*dee Ray-ni-goonk*	laundry and dry cleaning service

Whenever you're about to book a room at a hotel, don't let the giddiness you feel at being in a new country prevent you from asking a few important questions about your room. Is it quiet? Does it look out onto the courtyard or onto the street? Is it on a smoking floor or a nonsmoking floor? Are there extra blankets in the cupboard? Table 7.13 has some words you may find useful when cross-examining hotel receptionists.

Table 7.13 Hotel Basics

German	Pronunciation	English
das Badezimmer	*dAs bah-duh-tsi-muhR*	bathroom
das Dopplezimmer	*dAs do-pel-tsi-muhR*	double room
das Einzelzimmer	*dAs ayn-tsel-tsi-muhR*	single room
das Telefon	*dAs tey-ley-fon*	telephone
der Balkon	*deyR bAl-kohn*	balcony
der Farbfernseher	*deyR faRb-feRn-zay-heR*	color television

German	Pronunciation	English
der Fernseher	*deyR feRn-zay-heR*	television
der Safe	*deyR Zeyf*	safe
der Schlüssel	*deyR shlü-suhl*	key
der Wecker	*deyR ve-kuhR*	alarm clock
die Badewanne	*dee bah-duh-vA-nuh*	bathtub
die Dusche	*dee dew-shuh*	shower
die Halbpension	*dee hAlp-pen-zee-ohn*	just with breakfast
die Vollpension	*dee fol-pen-zee-ohn*	with meals
die Klimaanlage	*dee klee-mah-An-lah-guh*	air conditioning
die Toilette	*dee toee-le-tuh*	restroom
die Übernachtung	*dee üh-beR-nACH-toong*	overnight stay
ein Zimmer mit Aussicht	*ayn tsi-muhR mit ous-ziHt*	a room with a view
nach hinten	*nahCH hin-tuhn*	at the back
nach vorn	*nahCH foRn*	at the front
zum Garten	*tsoom gAR-tuhn*	on the garden
zum Hof	*tsoom hof*	on the courtyard
zur Meerseite	*tsewR meeR-zay-tuh*	on the sea

Numbers in Order Are Called Ordinal Numbers

The numbers used to refer to the floors of a building are known as *ordinal numbers*. An ordinal number refers to a specific number in a series. If your hotel is really fancy, there may be someone in the elevator who asks you, "Welcher Stock, bitte (*vel-HuhR shtok, bi-tuh*)?"

➤ Ordinal numbers are formed by adding *-te* to the numbers 2–19 and by adding *-ste* from 20 on. *Erste* (first), *dritte* (third), *siebte* (seventh), and *achte* (eighth) are exceptions.

➤ In English, we use letters (1st, 2nd, 3rd...), to express ordinal numbers. In German, use a period after the numeral: 1., 2., 3. and so on.

➤ Ordinal numbers take the gender (masculine, feminine, or neuter) and number (singular or plural) of the noun they modify.

Was haben Sie gesagt?

Ordinal Numbers Numbers that refer to a specific number in a series and answer the question, "Which one?"

Ordinal Numbers Decline, Too

Ordinal numbers take the weak declension when they come after *der* words (words such as *dieser, jener, jeder,* and so on). The weak declension of ordinal numbers is shown in the table that follows.

Case	Masuline	Singular Feminine	Neuter	Plural All Genders
Nom.	der erste	die erste	das erste	die ersten
Acc.	den ersten	die erste	das erste	die ersten
Dat.	dem ersten	der ersten	dem ersten	den ersten
Gen.	des ersten	der ersten	des ersten	der ersten

Ordinal numbers take the strong declension when they come after words that have no article (for example, the word in the sentence, "Zimmer 33, erstes Zimmer auf der rechten Seite, ist das schonste (Room 33, the first room on the right, is the most beautiful)."

Case	Masuline	Singular Feminine	Neuter	Plural All Genders
Nom.	erster	erste	erstes	erste
Acc.	ersten	erste	erstes	erste
Dat.	erstem	erster	erstem	ersten
Gen.	ersten	erster	ersten	erster

Ordinal numbers take the mixed declension when they precede *ein* words (words such as *ein, kein, mein, sein, ihr,* etc.). See the table that follows for the mixed declension of ordinal numbers:

Case	Masuline	Singular Feminine	Neuter	Plural All Genders
Nom.	ein erster	eine erste	ein erstes	die ersten
Acc.	einen ersten	eine erste	ein erstes	die ersten
Dat.	einem ersten	einer ersten	einem ersten	den ersten
Gen.	eines ersten	einer ersten	eines ersten	der ersten

Mixed Verbs Are Both Weak and Strong

Mixed verbs are called "mixed" because they have characteristics of both weak and strong verbs. In German, these verbs follow the conjugation of weak verbs in the present tense, and add -*te* endings to the past tense. But like strong verbs, the stem vowel of the infinitive in the past tense does not stay the same throughout the conjugation (and there is no set pattern of rules you can follow to conjugate them). Chapter 13 discusses the past tense and takes you through the conjugation of some mixed verbs. For now, keep in mind that the following verbs are mixed in German: *brennen* (*bRe-nuhn*), to burn; *bringen* (*bRin-guhn*), to bring; *denken* (*den-kuhn*), to think; *kennen* (*ke-nuhn*), to know a person or a place; *nennen* (*ne-nuhn*), to name; *rennen* (*Re-nuhn*), to run; *senden* (*sen-duhn*), to send; *wenden* (*ven-duhn*), to turn, to wind; *wissen* (*vi-suhn*), to know a fact.

Verbs with Prefixes

Pre means to come before and *fix* means to join onto or with; this is essentially what a prefix is—a series of letters (sometimes a word on its own) that you join onto the beginning of another word. Verbs with prefixes, referred to as *compound verbs*, are not a German phenomenon. In English there are many compound verbs: *to lead* and *to mislead*; *to rate, to overrate,* and *to underrate*; *to take, to mistake, to retake, to undertake,* and *to overtake.* In German as in English, the verb and the compound verb follow the same conjugation; *take* becomes *took* in the past tense, for example, and *mistake* becomes *mistook.*

There are two types of prefixes in German: Those that can be separated from the verb (separable) and those that cannot be separated from the verb (inseparable).

Was haben Sie gesagt?

Compound Verbs   Verbs that are formed by adding a prefix to the stem verb. In German, there are two types of compound verbs: those with separable prefixes and those with inseparable prefixes.

Sometimes a Verb Gets Separated from Its Prefix

When dealing with verbs with separable prefixes, keep the following in mind: Separable prefixes can be words on their own, usually adverbs or prepositions. Although in the infinitive form they appear to be one word, (as in the verb *weggehen,* which means "to go away"), the prefix functions separately in the sentence (*Er geht weg,* or, "He goes away,") and when the past participle is formed, the prefix precedes the *ge-,* as in, *Er ist weggegangen,* or "He went away." Again, you don't have to rack your brain over this now—you'll deal with past participle formation in Chapter 13.

Some common separable prefixes are *auf-, aus-, an-, bei-, mit-, nach-, vor-, weg-, weiter-, wieder-, zu-, zuruck-,* and *zusammen-.*

Was haben Sie gesagt?

When a prefix is separated from a compound verb, it occurs at the end of the clause, which also is often the end of the sentence: *Er geht jeden Morgen um sieben Uhr aus.*

Sometimes a Verb and Its Prefix Are Inseparable

There are nine prefixes that can be added to verbs to form compound verbs with inseparable prefixes. These are *be-, emp-, ent-, er-, ge-, miß-, ver-, wider-,* and *zer-.* Inseparable prefixes have the following characteristics: They cannot exist as separate words, they are always unstressed, and when verbs begin with them, the new compound verb does not take *ge-* to form the past participle (you'll learn about the formation of the past participle in Chapter 13). Some common verbs with inseparable prefixes are: *verstehen* (*feR-shtey-huhn*), to understand; *empfehlen* (*emb-fey-luhn*), to recommend; *vershprechen* (*feR-shpRe-Huhn*), to promise; *erfinden* (*eR-fin-duhn*), to invent.

Chapter 8

Weather: All Year Round

In This Chapter

➤ Weather conditions

➤ Days of the week

➤ Months of the year

➤ The four seasons

In this chapter, you'll pick up the vocabulary you need to understand the weather forecast and to make plans in a German city, inside or outside your hotel.

Is It Fahrenheit or Is It Celcius?

Americans in Germany have been laughed at leaving their hotels in 20-degree weather in heavy winter jackets. Why? The answer is simple: They misunderstood the weather forecast. Remember, Germans use Celsius (or Centigrade) not Fahrenheit, the way we do in the U.S. Twenty degrees in German weather terminology is actually 68 degrees Fahrenheit.

The phrases in Table 8.1 will come in handy when the topic is weather.

Sagen Sie mal...

To convert Fahrenheit to Celsius, subtract 32 from the Fahrenheit temperature and multiply the remaining number by .5. To convert Celsius to Fahrenheit, multiply the Celsius temperature by 1.8, then add 32.

Table 8.1   Weather Expressions

German	Pronunciation	English
Wie ist das Wetter?	*vee ist dAs ve-tuhR*	How is the weather?
Das Wetter ist furchtbar.	*dAs ve-tuhR ist fooRHt-bahR*	The weather is awful.
Das Wetter ist schlecht.	*dAs ve-tuhR ist shleCHt*	The weather is bad.
Das Wetter ist schön.	*dAs ve-tuhR ist shöhn*	The weather is beautiful.
Das Wetter ist schrecklich.	*dAs ve-tuhR ist shRek-liH*	The weather is horrible.
Es blitzt und donnert.	*es blitst oont do-nuhRt*	There is lightning and thunder.
Es gibt Regenschauer.	*es gipt rey-guhn-shou-uhR*	There are rain showers.
Es ist bewölkt.	*es ist buh-völkt*	It is cloudy.
Es ist böhig.	*es ist böh-hiH*	It is gusty.

German	Pronunciation	English
Es ist feucht.	*es ist foyHt*	It is humid.
Es ist heß.	*es ist hays*	It is hot.
Es ist heiter.	*es ist hay-tuhR*	It is clear.
Es ist kalt.	*es ist kAlt*	It is cold.
Es ist kühl.	*es ist kühl*	It is cool.
Es ist nebelig.	*es ist ney-bey-liH*	It is foggy.
Es ist regnerisch.	*es ist rek-nuh-Rish*	It is rainy.
Es ist stürmisch.	*es ist shtüR-mish*	It is stormy.
Es ist windig.	*es ist vin-diH*	It is windy.
Es regnet.	*es rek-nuht*	It is raining.
Es schneit.	*es shnayt*	It is snowing.
Es ist warm	*es ist vARm*	It is warm.
Es regnet sehr stark	*es Rek-nuht seyR shtARk*	It is raining hard.
Welche Temperatur ist es?	*vel-Huh temp-pey-rah-tewR ist es*	What's the temperature?
Es sind minus zehn Grad.	*es zint mee-noos tseyn gRaht*	It's minus ten degrees.
Es sind zehn Grad unter Null.	*es zint tseyn gRaht oon-tuhR nool*	It's ten degrees below zero.

Table 8.2 Weather Words

German	Pronunciation	English
der Nebel	*deyR ney-bel*	fog
bewölkt	*buh-völkt*	cloudy
der Hagel	*deyR hah-guhl*	hail
der Regen	*deyR Rey-guhn*	rain
der Schnee	*deyR shney*	snow
der Schneeregen	*deyR shney-Rey-guhn*	sleet
der Sprühregen	*deyR shpRüh-Rey-guhn*	drizzle

continues

Table 8.2 Continued

German	Pronunciation	English
die Regenschauer	*die Rey-guhn-shou-uhR*	showers
die Sonne	*dee zo-nuh*	sun
der Sturm	*deyR shtuRm*	storm
der Wind	*deyR vint*	wind
frisch	*fRish*	chilly
der klare Himmel	*deyR klah-Ruh hi-muhl*	clear sky
leicht	*layHt*	weak
leicht bewölkt	*layHt buh-völkt*	slightly cloudy
mäßig	*mäh-siH*	moderate
nebelig	*ney-bliH*	foggy
stark bewölkt	*shtARk buh-völkt*	very cloudy
stark	*shtARk*	strong
wechselhaft	*vek-sel-hAft*	changeable

And Today Is...

This section focuses on days, months, dates, and seasons.

Sonntag Means Sunday

Sonntag is Sunday, the day when—in Germany—all the stores are closed. Study the German names for the days of the week in Table 8.3.

Table 8.3 Days of the Week

German	Pronunciation	English
der Tag	*deyR tahk*	day
die Woche	*dee vo-CHuh*	week
Montag	*mon-tahk*	Monday
Dienstag	*dee-uhnts-tahk*	Tuesday
Mittwoch	*mit-voCH*	Wednesday

German	Pronunciation	English
Donnerstag	*do-nuhRs-tahk*	Thursday
Freitag	*fRay-tahk*	Friday
Samstag	*sAms-tahk*	Saturday
Sonntag	*son-tahk*	Sunday

To express *on* when talking about a specific day, Germans use the contraction *am,* a combination of the preposition *an* and *dem* (*dem* being the form the definite article *der* takes in the dative case):

> Am Montag gehe ich in die Stadt.
> *Am mohn-tahk gey-huh iH in dee shtAt*
> On Monday I go downtown.

To express that you do something on a specific day every week, simply add an *-s*, just as you do in English, to the end of the day:

> Montags gehe ich in die Stadt.
> *mohn-tahks gey-huh iH in dee shtat*
> On Mondays I go downtown.

January Is *Januar*

Now that you know how to chat about the weather you can ask friendly natives what the weather will be like in April, September, or even next month. All you need to learn is the months of the year (see Table 8.4).

Table 8.4   Months of the Year

German	Pronunciation	English
der Monat	*deyR moh-nAt*	month
das Jahr	*dAs yahR*	year
Januar	*yah-new-ahR*	January
Februar	*feb-Rew-ahR*	February

continues

Table 8.4   Continued

German	Pronunciation	English
März	*märts*	March
April	*A-pRil*	April
Mai	*mahee*	May
Juni	*yew-nee*	June
Juli	*yew-lee*	July
August	*ou-goost*	August
September	*sep-tem-buhR*	September
Oktober	*ok-toh-buhR*	October
November	*noh-vem-buhR*	November
Dezember	*dey-tsem-buhR*	December

To make clear that something is expected to happen *in* a particular month, use the contraction *im*, a combination of the preposition *in* and *dem* (which is the form *der* takes in the dative case):

In Köln, regnet es am stärksten im März.
in köln reyk-nuht es Am shtäRks-tuhn im märts
In Köln, it rains hardest in March.

Winter Is *der Winter*

As you engage in German conversations, there will be times when you'll want to talk about the seasons. Study the seasons in German in Table 8.5, and get ready to talk about summer, spring, winter, and fall.

Table 8.5   The Seasons of the Year

German	Pronunciation	English
die Jahreszeit	*dee yah-Ruhs-tsayt*	season
der Winter	*deyR vin-tuhR*	winter
der Frühling	*deyR fRüh-ling*	spring

German	Pronunciation	English
der Sommer	*deyR zo-muhR*	summer
der Herbst	*deyR heRpst*	autumn, fall

To express *in* when you are speaking of the seasons, the Germans use the contraction *im*:

> Im Winter fahre ich in die Alpen.
> *im vin-tuhR fah-Ruh iH in dee Al-puhn*
> I'm going to the Alps in the winter.

Dating Time

The Fourth of July, your own birthday, and the year you were first kissed: What do these things have in common? Well, if you want to chat about them, you've got to learn a few words that deal with dates. You can start with a few general terms in Table 8.6 dealing with chunks of time, like years and days.

Table 8.6 Years and Days

German	Pronunciation	English
eine Stunde	*ay-nuh shtoon-duh*	an hour
ein Tag	*ayn tahk*	a day
eine Woche	*ay-nuh vo-CHuh*	a week
ein Monat	*ayn moh-naht*	a month
ein Jahr	*ayn yahR*	a year
zwei Jahre	*tsvay yah-Ruh*	two years
einige Jahre	*ay-nee-guh yah-Ruh*	some years
nächstes Jahr	*näH-stuhs yahR*	next year
letztes Jahr	*lets-tuhs yahR*	last year

Writing a Date

Whether you have a dentist appointment or a romantic rendezvous, you will have to learn to express the date of the appointment differently than you do in the United States. Here is a formula for expressing the date correctly in German.

day of the week + *der* (cardinal) number + month + year

Montag, der dritte März 1997
mohn-tahk, deyR dRi-tuh mäRts 1997
Monday, the third of March 1997

You write and punctuate dates in German differently than you do in English. Compare the following date (May 6, 1997) in English and in German.

May 6, 1997 (5/6/97)
der 6. Mai 1997 (6.5.97)

When writing letters in German, the place from which you are writing is given first, followed by the date. Note that the accusative *den* is used when expressing a definite time.

New York, den 3.3.1997

Every day of the month is expressed using cardinal numbers: *der erste März, der zweite März, der dritte März,* and so on.

At first glance, the way you express the year in German looks like it could take a year to say. If you were to express the year 1997, for example, you would say:

neunzehnhundertsiebenundneunzig
noyn-tseyn-hoon-deRt-zee-buhn-oont-noyn-tsiH

or simply 97:

siebenundneunzig
zee-buhn-oont-noyn-tsiH

To get information about the date, you should be able to ask the following questions:

Welcher Tag ist heute?
vel-HuhR tahkist hoy-tuh
What day is today?

Der wievielte ist heute?
deyR vee-feel-tuhist hoy-tuh
What's today's date?

Was haben Sie gesagt?

Remember, the days of the week, months of the year, and the four seasons all take the masculine definite article *der*.

When someone answers your question, he will probably begin his response with one of the following:

Heute ist der …
hoy-tuh ist deyR …
Today is …

Achtung!

When writing dates, the sequence is day + month + year. In the United States the date generally starts with the month, followed by the day, and then the year. Note the differences in punctuation in German:

English	German
June 22, 1997	der 22 Juni 1997
6/22/97	22.6.97

Expressing Time

You don't always speak in terms of dates—sometimes you simply say, "in a week," or "a few days ago." There are many words you will need to know to schedule events, make plans, and arrange trysts. Study the expressions in Table 8.7.

Table 8.7   Time Expressions

German	Pronunciation	English
in	*in*	in
vor	*foR*	ago
nächste Woche	*näcH-stuh vo-Huh*	next week
letzte Woche	*lets-tuh vo-Huh*	last week
der Abend	*deyR ah-buhnd*	evening
vorgestern	*foR-ges-tuhRn*	day before yesterday
gestern	*ges-tuhRn*	yesterday
heute	*hoy-tuh*	today
morgen	*moR-guhn*	tomorrow
übermorgen	*üh-buhR-moR-guhn*	day after tomorrow
am nächsten Tag	*Am näH-stuhn tahk*	the next day
heute in einer Woche	*hoy-tuh in ay-nuh vo-Huh*	a week from today
heute in zwei Wochen	*hoy-tuh in tsvay vo-Huhn*	two weeks from today
der Morgen	*deyR moR-guhn*	morning
der Nachmittag	*deyR naH-mi-tahk*	afternoon

Chapter 9

Seeing the Sights

In This Chapter

➤ Enjoying the pleasures of sightseeing

➤ How to see what you want to see

➤ Making suggestions with modals

➤ More about prepositions

Now you are ready to venture out into a German, Swiss, or Austrian city, to explore the parks, the streets, or the shopping districts. After reading this chapter, not only will you be able to find your way around—you'll be well on your way to giving your opinions in German.

How to See What You Want to See

What's it going to be? The ancient rooms of a castle, the remains of the Berlin Wall, or the paintings in a museum? To express what you can see in a given place, you will need to use *man sieht* (*mAn zeet*), which means "one sees."

Remember that *sehen* is a strong verb. Complete conjugation for the present tense is given in Chapter 5.

The expression "man sieht…" is quite versatile—you can use it to talk about practically anything. Practice the following expressions.

> In Berlin sieht man das Brandenburger Tor.
> *in beR-leen zeet mAn dAs bRAn-den-booR-guhR toR*
> In Berlin, you see the Brandenburger Gate.

> Im Zirkus sieht man Elefanten.
> *im tsiR-koos zeet mAn ey-ley-fAn-tuhn*
> In the circus you see elephants.

> Im Kino sieht man einen Film.
> *im kee-no zeet mAn ay-nuhn film*
> In the cinema you see a movie.

Modals Are Kind of Like Having Kids

To make suggestions in German, you will need to use modals. *Modals* are verbs used in conjunction with other verbs, usually to form tenses other than the present. In the sentence, *Wir müssen nach Hause gehen,* for example, the modal verb *müssen* is the equivalent of *must*: "We must go home." This is different than saying, "We go home." Adding a modal to another verb is like having kids: Life is never the same again. These little guys modify the action of the main verb, (just like junior turns everything upside down), and significantly alter the meanings of sentences.

When a modal is used with another verb, it alters or modifies the other verb's meaning. The six principal modal auxiliary verbs in German are:

➤ *sollen* (*zo-luhn*), to ought to

➤ *müssen* (*mü-suhn*), to have to

➤ *dürfen* (*düR-fuhn*), to be allowed to

➤ *können* (*kö-nuhn*), to be able to

➤ *wollen* (*vo-luhn*), to want to

➤ *mögen* (*möh-guhn*), to like (something)

Because the present tense of modal auxiliary verbs is irregular, the best thing for you to do is to buckle down (grit your teeth a little, if you have to) and memorize the conjugations (see Tables 9.1 through 9.6).

Was haben Sie gesagt?

Modal Verbs A verb used with another verb to alter or modify its meaning. The six principal modal verbs in German are *sollen, müssen, dürfen, können, wollen,* and *mögen.*

Table 9.1   Conjugation of a Modal Auxiliary Verb: sollen

Person	Singular	English	Plural	English
First	ich soll *iH zol*	I ought to	wir sollen *veeR zo-luhn*	we ought to
Second	du sollst *dew zolst*	you ought to		
(Formal)	Sie sollen *zee zo-luhn*		ihr sollt *eeR zolt*	
Third	er, sie, es soll *eR, zee, es zol*	he, she, it ought to	sie sollen *zee zo-luhn*	they ought to

Table 9.2 Conjugation of a Modal Auxiliary Verb: mögen

Person	Singular	English	Plural	English
First	ich mag *iH mahk*	I like	wir mögen *veeR möh-guhn*	we like to
Second	du magst *dew mahkst*			
(Formal)	Sie mögen *zee möh-guhn*	you like	ihr mögt *eeR möhkt*	you like to
Third	er, sie, es mag *eR, zee, es mahk*	he, she, it likes	sie mögen *zee möh-guhn*	they like to

Table 9.3 Conjugation of a Modal Auxiliary Verb: dürfen

Person	Singular	English	Plural	English
First	ich darf *iH dARf*	I am allowed to	wir dürfen *veeR düR-fuhn*	we are allowed to
Second	du darfst *dew dARfst*	you are allowed to	ihr dürft *eeR düRft*	you are allowed to
(Formal)	Sie dürfen *zee düR-fuhn*		Sie dürfen *zee düR-fuhn*	
Third	er, sie, es darf *er, zee, es dARf*	he, she, it is allowed to	sie dürfen *zee düR-fuhn*	they are allowed to

Table 9.4 Conjugation of a Modal Auxiliary Verb: können

Person	Singular	English	Plural	English
First	ich kann *iH kAn*	I am able to	wir können *veeR kö-nuhn*	we are able to
Second	du kannst able to *dew kAnst*	you are	ihr könnt *eeR könt*	you are able to

Person	Singular	English	Plural	English
(Formal)	Sie können *zee kö-nuhn*		Sie können *zee kö-nuhn*	
Third	er, sie, es kann *er, zee, es kAn*	he, she, it is able to	sie können *zee kö-khn*	they are able to

Table 9.5 Conjugation of a Modal Auxiliary Verb: müssen

Person	Singular	English	Plural	English
First	ich muß *iH moos*	I have to	wir müssen *veeR mü-suhn*	we have to
Second	du mußt *dew moost*	you have to	ihr müst *eeR müst*	you have to
(Formal)	Sie müssen *zee mü-suhn*		Sie müssen *zee mü-suhn*	
Third	er, sie, es muß *er, zee, es moos*	he, she, it has to	sie müssen *zee mü-suhn*	they have to

Table 9.6 Conjugation of a Modal Auxiliary Verb: wollen

Person	Singular	English	Plural	English
First	ich will *iH vil*	I want to	wir wollen *veeR vo-luhn*	we want to
Second	du willst *dew vilst*	you want to	ihr wollt *eeR volt*	you want to
(Formal)	Sie wollen *zee vo-luhn*		Sie wollen *zee vo-luhn*	
Third	er, sie, es will *er, zee, es vil*	he, she, it wants to	sie wollen *zee vo-luhn*	they want to

Making Suggestions

To make suggestions in German, use the modals *sollen*, *dürfen, können,* or *wollen* plus the infinitive. If your suggestions don't seem to have an effect, use the modal *müssen* to express "must." Use *mögen* to express the things you like to do (on a regular basis). Note that the modal is conjugated and is in the second position in the sentence and that the verb carrying the meaning is placed in infinitive form at the end of the sentence.

sollen + gehen

German	Pronunciation	English
Sollen wir zum Fischmarkt gehen?	*zo-luhn veeR tsoom fish-mARkt gey-huhn*	Should we go to the fish market?
Wir sollen zum Fischmarkt gehen.	*veeR zo-luhn tsum fish-mARkt gey-huhn*	We should go to the fish market.

wollen + gehen

German	Pronunciation	English
Wollt ihr zum Fishmarkt gehen?	*volt eeR tsoom fish-mARkt gey-huhn*	Do you want to go to the fish market?
Wir wollen zum Fischmarkt gehen.	*veeR vo-luhn tsum fish-mARkt gey-huhn*	We want to go to the fish market.

mögen + gehen

German	Pronunciation	English
Magst du zum Fischmarkt gehen?	*mahkst dew tsoom fish-mARkt gey-huhn*	Do you like to go to the fishmarket?
Ich mag zum Fischmarkt gehen.	*iH mahk tsoom fishmARkt gey-huhn*	I like to go to the fishmarket.

müssen + gehen

German	Pronunciation	English
Müssen sie zum Fishmarkt gehen?	*veeR mü-suhn tsoom fish-mARkt gey-hun*	Must they go to the fishmarket?
Sie müssen zum Fischmarkt gehen.	*zee mü-suhn tsum fish-mARkt gey-huhn*	They must go to the fishmarket.

dürfen + gehen

German	Pronunciation	English
Darf ich zum Fischmarkt gehen?	*dARf iH tsoom fish-mARkt gey-huhn*	Am I allowed to go to the fishmarket?
Ich darf zum Fischmarkt gehen.	*iH dARf tsoom fish-mARkt gey-huhn*	I'm allowed to go to the fishmarket.

können + gehen

German	Pronunciation	English
Können wir nach Hause gehen?	*kö-nuhn veeR nahCH hou-suh gey-huhn*	Can we go home?
Wir können nach Hause gehen.	*veeR kö-nuhn nahCH hou-suh gey-huhn*	We can go home.

How to Respond to Suggestions

In the following sections, you'll be introduced to some common ways of responding to suggestions.

Say "Yes" or "No"—and Then Some

If you're irritated at whomever is making a given suggestion, by all means answer him with a brusque, "Yes," or "No." Otherwise, you may want to take a somewhat gentler approach and decline a suggestion with, "Yes, but...," or "No, because..."

Ja, es interesiert mich...
yah, es in-tuh-Re-seeRt miH
Yes, I'm interested...

Nein, es interesiert mich nicht...
nayn, es in-tuh-Re-seeRt miH niHt
No, I'm not interested...

Ja, ich bin daran interesiert...
yah, ich bin dah-RAn in-tuh-Re-seeRt
Yes, I'm interested...

Nein, ich bin nicht daran interesiert...
nayn, iH bin niHt dah-RAn in-tuh-Re-seeRt
No, I'm not interested...

Ja, es sagt mir zu...
ya, es zahkt meeR tsoo
Yes, I'd like to...

Nein, es sagt mir nicht zu...
nayn, es zahkt meeR niHt tsoo
No, I wouldn't like to...

To express boredom, dislike, or disgust say:

German	Pronunciation	English
Ich mag...nicht.	*iH mahk...niHt*	I don't like...
Ich hasse...	*iH hA-suh*	I hate...
Ich verabschaue...	*iH feR-ap-shoy-uh*	I abominate...
Es ist langweilig.	*es ist lAnk-vay-liH*	It's boring.
Das ist grauenhaft.	*das ist gRou-en-hAft*	That is horrible.

Saying What You Think

When someone suggests that the two of you go to the opera and the suggestion appeals to you, answer him with, "Ich finde die Oper toll." If you begin your answers with "Ich finde," you can be pretty much assured that you're going to be saying something that makes sense. Here are some alternative ways to show your enthusiasm:

> Ich liebe die Oper!
> *iH lee-buh dee o-puhR*
> I love opera!

> Ich mag die Oper.
> *iH mahk dee oh-puhR*
> I like opera.

To express joy, excitement, or anticipation at doing something, give your positive opinion by saying:

> IEs ist…
> *es ist*
> It is…

> Das ist…
> *dAs ist*
> That is…

Here are some common German superlatives:

German	Pronunciation	English
fantastisch!	*fAn-tAs-tish*	fantastic!
schön!	*shöhn*	beautiful!
wunderschön!	*voon-deR-shöhn*	wonderful!
super!	*zew-puhR*	super!
unglaublich!	*oon-gloup-liH*	unbelievable!
atemberaubend!	*ah-tuhm-be-Rou-buhnt*	breathtaking!
sensationell!	*zen-zah-tseeon-el*	sensational!

Chapter 10

Let's Go Shopping

In This Chapter

➤ Clothing, colors, sizes, materials, and designs

➤ Demonstrative adjectives: this, that, these, and those

➤ Direct object pronouns

➤ Going out for the evening

Whether you love it or hate it, this chapter will help you make the right decisions when you shop.

At the Store

One of the least expensive (and, for some, most enjoyable) ways to shop is with your eyes. Table 10.1 will start you on your way to guilt-free browsing in your favorite German stores (*die Geschäfte*).

Table 10.1 Stores

Store	What You Can Buy There
das Bekleidunggeschäft (*dAs be-klay-doonks-guh-shäft*) clothing store	die Bekleidung, f., (*dee buh-klay-doong*): clothes
das Blumengeschäft (*dAs blew-muhn-guh-shäft*) florist	die Blumen, f., (*dee blew-muhn*): flowers
das Lederwarengeschäft (*dAs ley-deR-vah-Ren-guh-shäft*) leather goods store	die Gürtel, m., (*dee güR-tuhl*), die Lederjacken, f., (*dee ley-deR-yA-kuhn*), die Geldbörsen, f., (*dee gelt-böR-zuhn*): belts, leather jackets, wallets
das Musikgeschäft (*dAs mew-zik-guh-shäft*) music store	die CDs, f., (*dee tse-des*), die Kassetten, f., (*dee kA-se-tuhn*): CDs, tapes
das Sportgeschäft (*dAs shpoRt-guh-shäft*) sport shop	die Sportbekleidung, f., (*dee shpoRt-buh-klay-doong*), die Turnschuhe, m., (*dee tooRn-shew-huh*), die Sportgeräte, n., (*dee shpoRt-guh-Räh-tuh*): sports clothing, sneakers, sports equipment
der Geschenkartikelladen (*deyR guh-shenk-AR-ti-kuhl-lah-duhn*) gift shop	die Miniaturdenkmähler, n., (*dee mee-nee-ah-tooR-denk-mäh-luhR*), die T-shirts, n., (*dee tee-shiRts*), die Stadtpläne, m., (*dee shtAt-pläh-nuh*): miniature monuments, T-shirts, maps
der Kiosk (*deyR kee-osk*) newsstand	die Zeitungen, f., (*dee tsay-toon-guhn*), die Zeitschriften, f., (*dee tsayt-shRif-tuhn*): newspapers, magazines
der Schallplattenladen (*deyR shAl-plA-tuhn-lah-duhn*) record store	die Schallplatten, f., (*shAl-plA-tuhn*): records, CDs
der Tabakladen (*deyR tA-bAk-lah-duhn*) tobacconist	die Zigaretten, f., (*dee tsee-gah-Re-tuhn*) die Zigarren, f., (*dee tsee-gA-Ruhn*), die Feuerzeuge, n., (*dee foy-uhR-tsoy-guh*): cigarettes, cigars, lighters
die Apotheke (*dee A-po-tey-kuh*) pharmacy	die Medikamente, n., (*dee meh-dih-kah-men-tuh*) medicine
die Buchhandlung (*dee bewCH-hAn-dloong*) bookstore	die Bücher, n., (*dee bü-CHuhR*): books

Store	What You Can Buy There
die Drogerie (*dee dRoh-guh-Ree*) drug store	die Schönheitsartikel, m., (*dee shön-hayts-Ar-tih-kuhl*) beauty articles
die Papierwarenhandlung (*dee pah-peeR-wah-Ruhn hAn-dloong*) stationery store	die Stifte, m., (*dee shtif-tuh*), die Schreibwaren, f., (*dee shRayp-vah-Ruhn*):pens, stationery
die Parfümerie (*dee pAR-fü-muh-Ray*) perfume store	das Parfüm, (*dAs paR-füm*):perfume
das Schmuckgeschäft (*dAs shmook-guh-shäft*) jewelry store	der Schmuck (*deyR shmook*):jewelry

Getting Dressed in Düsseldorf

If you happen to visit Münich or Düsseldorf, you may want to check out the clothing stores. The vocabulary in Table 10.2 will help you purchase something in the latest fashion, or *in der neusten Mode* (*in deyR noy-stuhn moh-duh*).

Table 10.2 Clothing

German	Pronunciation	English
das Hemd	*dAs hemt*	shirt
das Kleid	*dAs klayt*	dress
das T-shirt	*dAs tee-shöRt*	T-shirt
der Anzug	*deyR An-tsewk*	suit
der Büstenhalter	*deyR bü-stuhn-hAl-tuhR*	bra
der Gürtel	*deyR güR-tuhl*	belt
der Hut	*deyR hewt*	hat
der Pullover	*deyR pool-oh-vuhR*	pullover
der Regenmantel	*deyR Rey-guhn-mAn-tuhl*	raincoat

continues

Table 10.2 Continued

German	Pronunciation	English
der Rock	*deyR Rok*	skirt
der Schal	*deyR shahl*	scarf
der Schlafanzug	*deyR shlahf-An-tsook*	pajamas
der Schlüpfer	*deyR shlüp-fuhR*	briefs
die Handschuhe	*dee hAnt-schew-huh*	gloves
die Hose	*dee hoh-zuh*	pants
die Jacke	*dee yA-kuh*	jacket
die Jeans	*dee jeens*	jeans
die Krawatte	*dee kRah-vA-tuh*	tie
die kurze Hose	*dee kooR-tsuh hoh-zuh*	shorts
die Mütze	*dee mü-tsuh*	cap
die Schuhe	*dee shew-huh*	shoes
die Socken (pl.)	*dee zo-kuhn*	socks
die Strumpfhose	*dee shtRoompf-hoh-zuh*	tights
die Turnschuhe	*dee tooRn-shew-huh*	sneakers
die Unterhose	*dee oon-tuhR-hoh-zuh*	underpants

You Wear It Well: The Verb *tragen*

Now that you've bought what you wanted, wear it out—
in German. Table 10.3 helps you express the concept
of wearing clothing with the verb *tragen* (*tRah-guhn*),
to wear.

Table 10.3 The Verb tragen

Person	Singular	English	Plural	English
First	ich trage *iH tRah-guh*	I wear	wir tragen *veeR tRah-guhn*	we wear
Second	du trägst *dew tRähkst*	you wear	ihr tragt *eeR tRahkt*	you wear

Person	Singular	English	Plural	English
(Formal)	Sie tragen *zee tRah-guhn*		Sie tragen *zee tRah-guhn*	
Third	er, sie, es tragen *eR, zee, es tRah-guhn*	he, she, it wears	sie tragen *zee tRah-guhn*	they wear

Colorful German

Certain colors are associated with certain moods or states of being. Don't be too quick to use the colors in Table 10.4 figuratively—at least not in the same way you would use them in English. "Er ist blau (*eR ist blou*)," which translates into English as, "He is blue," does not mean "He is sad." Germans use this phrase to indicate that someone has had too much too drink. However you use them, the colors (*die Farben*) in Table 10.4 will help you in your description of people, places, and things.

Table 10.4   Colors

German	Pronunciation	English
beige	*beyj*	beige
blau	*blou*	blue
braun	*bRoun*	brown
gelb	*gelp*	yellow
grau	*gRou*	gray
grün	*gRün*	green
lilac	*lee-lah*	purple
orange	*oR-An-juh*	orange
rosa	*Roh-zah*	pink
rot	*Rot*	red
schwarz	*shvaRts*	black
weiß	*vays*	white

To describe any color as light, simply add the word *hell* (*hel*) as a prefix to the color to form a compound adjective:

hellrot	hellgrün	hellblau
hel-Rot	*hel-gRün*	*hel-blou*
light red	light green	light blue

To describe a color as dark, add the word *dunkel* (*doon-kuhl*) as a prefix to the color to form a compound adjective:

dunkelrot	dunkelgrün	dunkelblau
doon-kuhl-Rot	*doon-kuhl-gRün*	*doon-kuhl-blou*
dark red	dark green	dark blue

To express need or desire, you can use *möchten*, which—although it is the subjunctive form of the modal verb *mögen*—is often used as a present tense verb on its own. "Ich möchte" is the equivalent of "I would like." Don't confuse it with *mögen*, which means "to like (something)." You can make a big mistake by confusing the two. If you're in a clothing store and you say "Ich möchte Kleider" (I would like some dresses), instead of "Ich mag Kleider" (I like dresses), you might end up with an armful of dresses and be expected to try them on, whether you're in the mood for trying on dresses or not.

Fabric Choices

Table 10.5 will help you pick the material (die Materialien) you prefer when you shop.

Table 10.5   Materials

German	Pronunciation	Meaning
das Leder	*dAs ley-deR*	leather
das Leinen	*dAs lay-nuhn*	linen
das Nylon	*dAs nay-lon*	nylon
das Polyester	*dAs poh-lee-es-tuhR*	polyester
das Wildleder	*dAs vilt-ley-deR*	suede

German	Pronunciation	Meaning
der Flanell	*deyR flah-nel*	flannel
der Kaschmir	*deyR kAsh-meeR*	cashmere
der Kord	*deyR koRt*	corduroy
der Stoff	*deyR shtof*	denim
die Baumwolle	*dee boum-wo-luh*	cotton
die Seide	*dee zay-duh*	silk
die Wolle	*dee vo-luh*	wool

If you want to express that you want something made out of a certain material, you would use the preposition *aus*.

Ich möchte ein Kleid aus Seide.
iH möH-tuh ayn klayt ous zay-duh
I'd like a silk dress.

Pronouns Affected by Cases!

In Chapter 4, you learned about the accusative (direct object) and dative (indirect object) case relative to nouns. Now you're going to see how these cases affect pronouns.

If one of your friends told you that she loves her favorite pair of shoes and that she wears her favorite pair of shoes all the time and that she only takes her favorite pair of shoes off when she get blisters from dancing too much, you would probably want to take off one of *your* shoes and hit her over the head with it. She could be less long-winded if she stopped repeating "favorite pair of shoes" (a direct object noun in English) and replaced it with "them" (a direct object pronoun in English). In German, the direct object is in the accusative case and is often called the accusative object. The indirect object is in the dative case and called the dative object. If you've forgotten what you learned about cases in Chapter 4, this should refresh your memory.

Nouns or pronouns in the accusative case answer the question whom or what the subject is acting on and can refer to people, places, things, or ideas.

	Nominative (Subj.)	Verb	Accusative (Direct Obj.)
With Noun	Ich (I)	trage (wear)	meine Lieblingsschuhe. (my favorite shoes)
With Pronoun	Ich (I)	trage (wear)	sie. (them)
With Noun	Sie (they)	lieben (love)	das Leben. (life)
With Pronoun	Sie (they)	lieben (love)	es. (it)

Indirect object nouns or pronouns (in German, nouns or pronouns in the dative case) answer the question to whom or to what the action of the verb is being performed.

	Nominative (Subj.)	Verb	Accusative (Indirect Obj.)	Dative (Direct Obj.)
With Noun	Ich (I)	kaufe (buy)	meinem Freund (my friend)	eine Mütze. (a cap)
With Pronoun	Ich (I)	kaufe (buy)	ihm (him)	eine Mütze. (a cap)
With Noun	Sie (she)	gibt (gives)	ihrer Schwester (her sister)	ein Geschenk. (a gift)
With Pronoun	Sie (she)	gibt (gives)	ihr (her sister)	ein Geschenk. (a gift)

In English, direct and indirect pronouns are used to avoid repeating the same nouns over and over again. In German, direct object pronouns are in the accusative case and indirect object pronouns are in the dative case. Table 10.6 provides you with a comprehensive chart of pronouns in German and what they stand for (D.O. stands for "direct object" and I.O. stands for "indirect object").

Table 10.6   Singular Object Pronouns

D. O. Pronouns	English	I. O. Pronouns	English
mich (*miH*)	me	mir (*meeR*)	to me
dich (*diH*)	you	dir (*deeR*)	to you
Sie (*zee*)	you	Ihnen (*ee-nuhn*)	to you (Formal)
ihn (*een*)	him, it	ihm (*eem*)	to him
sie (*zee*)	her, it	ihr (*eeR*)	to her
es* (*es*)	it	ihm (*eem*)	to it

Es is used as a direct object pronoun for neuter nouns, most of which are things. There are, however, a few exceptions. *Es* means "her," for example, in the sentence *Ich liebe es,* when *es* refers to *das Mädchen.*

Table 10.7   Plural Object Pronouns

D. O. Pronouns	English	I. O. Pronouns	English
uns (*oons*)	us	uns (*oons*)	to us
euch (*oyH*)	you	euch (*oyH*)	to you
Sie (*zee*)	you	Ihnen (*ee-nuhn*)	to you (Formal)
sie (*zee*)	them	ihnen (*ee-nuhn*)	to them

Sagen Sie mal...

When dealing with neuter nouns ending in *-chen* or *-lein*, you can use either the pronoun *es* (following the grammatical gender) or you can use the pronoun *er* or *sie* depending on the logical gender of the noun.

Was mach Ihr Söhnchen?

Es (or er) geht...

Das Mädchen will nicht mehr singen.

Es (or Sie) is müde.

Where to Position Those Object Pronouns

In swank social circles, position is everything. It's the same with direct and indirect objects in German. When both the direct and indirect objects of a sentence are pronouns, the direct object comes first, followed by the indirect object.

Ich schreibe dem Vater eine Postkarte.
iH shRay-buh deym fah-tuhR ay-nuh post-kAR-tuh
I write a postcard to the father.

Ich schreibe sie ihm.
iH shRay-buh zee eem
I write it to him.

When either the direct or indirect object pronoun is a noun, however, the pronoun always comes first—no matter what case it's in.

Ich schreibe ihm eine Postkarte.
iH shRay-buh eem ay-nuh post-kAR-tuh
I write him a postcard.

Achtung!

Remember, *ihn* and *ihm* are used for nouns with the masculine noun marker *der*; *sie* and *ihr* are used for nouns with the feminine noun marker *die*; and *es* and *ihm* are used for nouns with the neuter noun marker *das*. For masculine, feminine, and neuter nouns with the plural noun maker *die* use *sie* for direct object pronouns and *ihnen* for indirect object pronouns.

Direct Object	Indirect Object
Ich schreibe einen Brief. *iH shRay-buh ay-nuhn bReef* I write a letter.	Ich spreche mit Stefan. *iH shpRe-Huh mit shte-fahn* I talk to Stefan.
Ich schreibe ihn. *iH shRay-buh een* I write it.	Ich spreche mit ihm. *iH shpRe-Huh mit eem* I talk to him.
Ich schreibe ihn nicht. *iH shRay-buh een niHt* I don't write it.	Ich spreche nicht mit ihm. *iH shpRe-Huh niHt mit eem* I don't talk to him.
Ich werde ihn schreiben. *iH veR-duh een shray-buhn* I will write it.	Ich werde nicht mit ihm sprechen. *iH veR-duh niHt mit eem shpRe-Huhn* I won't talk to him.
Schreibe ihn nicht! *shRay-buh een niHt* Don't write it!	Sprich nicht mit ihm! *shpRiH niHt mit eem* Don't talk to him!

You Can Always Get What You Want—if You Know How to Ask

Here are some phrases to help you through the most common in-store shopping situations:

Kann ich Ihnen helfen?
kAn iH ee-nuhn hel-fuhn
May I help you?

Was wünschen Sie?
vAs vün-shuhn zee
What would you like?

Nein danke, ich schaue mich nur um.
nayn dAn-kuh, iH shou-uh miH nooR oom
No, thank you, I am (just) looking.

Ja, ich würde gern...sehen.
yah, iH vüR-duh geRn...sey-huhn
Yes, I would like to see...

Ich such...
iH zew-CHuh...
I'm looking for...

Haben sie einen Schlußverkauf?
hah-buhn zee ay-nuhn shloos-veR-kouf
Do you have an end-of-season sale?

This and That: Being Selective

There's absolutely nothing wrong with asking your sales-person (or the cashier, or anyone else within asking distance) what he or she thinks of a particular article you are considering adding to you wardrobe. To ask someone his or her opinion about a suit, tie, hat, or skirt, you'll need to use a demonstrative pronoun (sometimes referred to as demonstrative adjectives). *Demonstrative pronouns* such as *dieser* (this) and *jener* (that) allow you to be specific about whatever it is you're pointing out. The important thing to remember is that in German, demonstrative pronouns must agree in number, gender, and case. In Table 10.8, *dieser* is declined in all four cases. *Jener* follows the same declension.

Table 10.8   Demonstrative Pronouns: This, That, These, Those

Case	Masculine	Feminine	Neuter	Plural All Genders
Nom.	dieser Hut *dee-zuhR hewt*	diese Hose *dee-zuh hoh-suh*	dieses Kleid *dee-zuhs klayt*	diese *dee-zuh*
Acc.	diesen Hut *dee-zuhn hewt*	diese Hose *dee-zuh hoh-zuh*	dieses Kleid *dee-zuhs klayt*	diese *dee-zuh*
Dat.	diesem Hut *dee-zuhm hewt*	dieser Hose *dee-zuhR hoh-zuh*	diesem Kleid *de-zuhm klayt*	diesen *dee-zuhn*
Gen.	dieses Huts *dee-suhs hewts*	dieser Hose *dee-zuhR*	dieses Kleids *dee-zuhs klayts*	dieser *dee-zuhR*

What Do YOU Think?

German	Pronunciation	English
Das gefällt mir.	*dAs guh-fält miR*	I like it.
Das steht mir gut.	*dAs shteyt miR gewt*	That suits me well.
Es ist angenehm.	*es ist An-guh-neym*	It's nice.
Es ist elegant.	*es ist ey-ley-gAnt*	It's elegant.
Es ist praktisch.	*es ist pRAk-tish*	It's practical.
Es gefällt mir nicht.	*es guh-fält miR niHt*	I don't like it.
Das steht mir nicht.	*dAs shteyt miR niHt*	That doesn't suit me.
Es ist schrecklich.	*es ist shRek-liH*	It's horrible.
Es ist zu klein.	*es ist zew klayn*	It's too small.
Es ist zu groß.	*es ist zew gRohs*	It's too big.
Es ist zu eng.	*es ist zew eng*	It's too tight.
Es ist zu lang.	*es ist zew lAng*	It's too long.
Es ist zu kurz.	*es ist zew kooRts*	It's too short.
Es ist zu schrill.	*es ist zew shRil*	It's too loud.

Expressing Your Choices

Many questions concerning style and size begin with the interrogative pronoun *welcher*, which you were introduced to in Chapter 7. *Welcher* follows the same declension as the demonstrative pronoun *dieser* shown in Table 10.8.

Sample Question:

> Welches Hemd gefällt Ihnen am besten?
> *vel-Huhs hemt guh-fält ee-nuhn Am bes-tuhn*
> Which shirt do you like best?

Answer:

> Dieses Hemd dort gefällt mir am besten.
> *dee-suhs hemt doRt guh-fält miR Am bes-tuhn*
> I like that shirt there best.

Was haben Sie gesagt?

Demonstrative Pronouns Pronouns such as *dieser* (this) and *jener* (that) that allow you to be specific by pointing out someone or something.

And After You're Finished Shopping...It's Time for Fun!

To tell someone you'd like to do something, use the verb *mögen (möh-guhn)* in the subjunctive mood: *ich möchte (iH möH-tuh)*, conjugated in Table 10.9. This is the equivalent of saying, "I would like."

Table 10.9 The Verb mögen in the Subjunctive

Person	Singular	English	Plural	English
First	ich möchte *iH möH-tuh*	I would like	wir möchten *veeR möH-tuhn*	we would like
Second	du möchtest *dew möH-test*	you would like	ihr möchtet *eeR möH-tuht*	you would like
(Formal)	Sie möchten *zie möH-tuhn*		Sie möchten *zie möH-tuhn*	
Third	er, sie, es möchte *eR, zee, es möH-tuh*	he, she, it would like	sie möchten *zee möH-tuhn*	they would like

There are many reliable ways of having a good time, and new ways are being invented every day. Tables 10.10 and 10.11 list several possibilities. To tell someone that you would like to go to the opera, you might say:

> Ich möchte in die Oper gehen.
> *IH möH-tuh in dee oh-puhR gey-huhn*
> I would like to go to the opera.

If you'd like to go to the movies, you could say:

> Ich möchte ins Kino gehen.
> *IH möH-tuh ins kee-moh gey-huhn*
> I'd like to go to the movies.

Table 10.10 Places to Go

Place	English
Zum Strand gehen *tsoom stRAnt gey-huhn*	to go to the beach
Ins Ballet gehen *ins bA-let gey-huhn*	to go the ballet
Ins Kasino gehen *ins kah-zee-noh gey-huhn*	to go to the casino

continues

Table 10.10   Continued

Place	English
Ins Theater gehen *ins tey-ah-tuhR gey-huhn*	to go to the theater
Ins Konzert gehen *ins kon-tseRt gey-huhn*	to go to a concert

Table 10.11   Things to Do

Activity	English
schwimmen, sich sonnen *shvi-muhn, siH zo-nuhn*	to swim, to lie in the sun
die Tänzer anschauen *dee tän-tsuhR An-shou-uhn*	to watch the dancers
spielen *shpee-luhn*	to play
ein Theaterstück sehen *ayn tey-ah-tuRh-shtük zey-huhn*	to see a play
ein Orchester hören *ayn oR-kes-tuhR höh-Ruhn*	to hear a concert

Chapter 11

Food for Thought

In This Chapter

➤ Buying food and reading a wine label

➤ How to order in a restaurant, bar, or café

➤ How to get what you want, exactly the way you want it

➤ Special diets

What do you feel like? You could get a sandwich (*ein belegtes Brot, ayn bey-lek-tuhs bRoht*) at a café (*das Cafe, dAs kah-fey*), or stop in a supermarket (*der Supermarkt, deyR zew-peR-mARkt*) for bread (*das Brot, dAs bRoht*) and cheese (*der Käse, deyR käh-zuh*) and make your own. This chapter will help you get the food you want in just the right amount.

Making Your Own Lunch

The list of foods and food shops in Table 11.1 should help you keep your appetite sated while you shop and sightsee.

Table 11.1   Foods and Food Shops

German	Pronunciation	English
das Fischgeschäft	*dAs fish-guh-shäft*	fish store
das Fleisch	*dAs flaysh*	meat
das Gebäck	*dAs guh-bäk*	pastry (sweet)
das Gemüse	*dAs guh-müh-zuh*	vegetables
das Lebensmittelgeschäft	*dAs ley-buhns-mi-tuhl-guh-shäft*	grocery store
der Fisch	*deyR fish*	fish
der Nachtisch	*deyR nahCH-tish*	dessert
der Supermarkt	*deyR zew-peR-mARkt*	supermarket
der Wein	*deyR vayn*	wine
die Bäckerei	*dee bä-kuh-Ray*	bakery
die Früchte	*dee fRüH-tuh*	fruits
die Metzgerei	*dee mets-guh-Ray*	butcher shop
die Spirituosen	*dee Spee-Ree-too-oh-zuhn*	liquors
die Weinhandlung	*dee vayn-hAnt-loong*	wine store

Shopping the Food Stalls

You've familiarized yourself with all the food and pastry shops near your hotel. You're armed with nothing but your appetite and a few *Deutsche Mark*. When it's time to go out into the world for whatever it is you need to stock your miniature hotel refrigerator, use the verb *gehen* and the preposition *zu* + the correctly declined definite article (see Chapter 4 for the declension of nouns) to indicate the store you're about to ambush. Keep in mind that the preposition *zu* is always followed by the dative case.

Preposition and Article	Contraction	Example	English
zu + dem=	zum	Ich gehe zum Supermarkt. *iH gey-huh tsoom zew-peR-mARkt*	I go to the supermarket.
zu + der=	zur	Ich gehe zur Weinhandlung. *iH gey-huh tsooR vayn-hant-loong*	I go to the liquor store.

Table 11.2 At the Grocery Store

German	Pronunciation	English
das Sauerkraut	*dAs zou-eR-kRout*	pickled cabbage
der Kohl	*deyR kohl*	cabbage
der Kohlrabi	*deyR kohl-Rah-bee*	turnip
der Kopfsalat	*deyR Kopf-zah-laht*	lettuce
der Mais	*deyR mays*	corn
der Pfeffer	*deyR pfe-fuhR*	pepper
der Pilz	*deyR pilts*	mushroom
der Reis	*deyR Rays*	rice
der Sellerie	*deyR ze-luh-Ree*	celery
der Spargel	*deyR shpAR-guhl*	asparagus
der Spinat	*deyR spee-naht*	spinach
die Aubergine	*dee oh-beR-jee-nuh*	eggplant
die Bohne	*dee boh-nuh*	bean
die Erbse	*dee eRp-suh*	pea
die Essiggurke	*dee e-siH-gooR-kuh*	sour pickle
die Gurke	*dee gooR-kuh*	cucumber
die Kartoffel	*dee kAr-to-fuhl*	potato
die Karotte	*dee kah-ro-tuh*	carrot

continues

Table 11.2 Continued

German	Pronunciation	English
die Radieschen (pl.)	*dee RA-dees-Huhn*	radishes
die Tomate	*dee toh-mah-tuh*	tomato
die Zweibel	*dee zvee-buhl*	onion
gemischtes Gemüse	*ge-mish-tuhs guh-müh-zuh*	mixed vegetables

Table 11.3 At the Fruit Store

German	Pronunciation	English
das Obst	*dAs opst*	fruits
der Apfel	*deyR Ap-fel*	apple
der Pfirsich	*deyR pfeeR-ziH*	peach
die Annanas	*dee A-nah-nAs*	pineapple
die Aprikose	*dee Ap-Ree-koh-zuh*	apricot
die Banane	*dee bah-nah-nuh*	banana
die Birne	*dee beeR-nuh*	pear
die Blaubeere	*dee blou-bey-Ruh*	blueberry
die Erdbeere	*dee eRt-bey-Ruh*	strawberry
die Himmbeere	*dee him-bey-Ruh*	raspberry
die Johannesbeere	*dee yoh-hA-nis-bey-Ruh*	currant
die Kastanie	*dee kAs-tah-nee-uh*	chestnut
die Kirsche	*dee keeR-shuh*	cherry
die Mandel	*dee mAn-duhl*	almond
die Melone	*dee mey-loh-nuh*	melon
die Nüsse	*dee nü-suh*	nuts
die Orange	*dee oh-RAn-juh*	orange
die Pampelmuse	*dee pAm-puhl-mew-zuh*	grapefruit
die Pflaume	*dee pflou-muh*	prune

German	Pronunciation	English
die Preiselbeere	*dee pRay-suhl-bey-Ruh*	cranberry
die Rosine	*dee Roh-zee-nuh*	grape
die Wassermelone	*dee vA-suhR-mey-loh-nuh*	watermelon
die Zitrone	*dee tsee-tRoh-nuh*	lemon

Table 11.4 At the Butcher or Delicatessen

German	Pronunciation	English
das Fleisch	*dAs flaysh*	meat
das Huhn	*dAs hewn*	chicken
das Kalbfleisch	*dAs kAlp-flaysh*	veal
das Kaninchen	*dAs kah-neen-Huhn*	rabbit
das Lamm	*dAs lAm*	lamb
das Rindfleisch	*dAs Rint-flaysh*	beef
das Schnitzel	*dAs shnit-suhl*	cutlet
das Wienerschnitzel	*dAs vee-nuhR-shnit-suhl*	breaded veal cutlet
der Hammelbraten	*deyR hA-mel-bRah-tuhn*	roast mutton
der Hase	*deyR hah-zuh*	hare
der Hasenbraten	*deyR hah-zuhn-bRah-tuhn*	roast hare
der Hirschbraten	*deyR hiRsh-bRah-tuhn*	venison
der Königsberger Klops	*deyR köh-niks-beR-guhR klops*	meatball in caper sauce
der Rehrücken	*deyR Rey-Rü-kuhn*	saddle of venison
der Rinderbraten	*deyR Rin-deR-bRah-tuhn*	roast beef
der Schinken	*deyR shin-kuhn*	ham
der Speck	*deyR shpek*	bacon
der Truthahn	*deyR tRewt-hahn*	turkey
die Bratwurst	*dee bRaht-vooRst*	fried sausage

continues

Table 11.4 Continued

German	Pronunciation	English
die Ente	*dee en-tuh*	duck
die Gans	*dee gants*	goose
die Leber	*dee ley-buhR*	liver
die Wurst	*dee vooRst*	sausage

Table 11.5 At the Fish Store

German	Pronunciation	English
der Fisch	*deyR fish*	fish
der Hummer	*deyR hoo-muhR*	lobster
der Kabeljau	*deyR kah-bel-you*	cod
der Krebs	*deyR kReyps*	crab
der Lachs	*deyR lAks*	salmon
der Tintenfish	*deyR tin-tuhn-fish*	squid
der Tunfisch	*deyR tewn-fish*	tuna
die Auster	*dee ous-tuhR*	oyster
die Flunder/ der Rochen	*dee floon-duhR/ deyR Ro-CHuhn*	flounder
die Forelle	*dee foh-Re-luh*	trout
die Froschschenkel (m.)	*dee fRosh-shen-kuhl*	frog legs
die Garnele	*dee gahR-ney-luh*	shrimp
die Krabben (f.)	*dee kRA-buhn*	shrimp, prawns
die Sardine	*dee zAR-dee-nuh*	sardine
die Scholle	*dee sho-luh*	flatfish
die Seezunge	*dee zey-tsoon-guh*	sole

Table 11.6 At the Dairy

German	Pronunciation	English
das Ei, die Eier (pl.)	*dAs ay, dee ay-eR*	eggs
der Käse	*deyR käh-zuh*	cheese
der Yoghurt	*der yoh-gooRt*	yogurt
die Butter	*dee boo-tuhR*	butter
die Magermilch	*dee mah-guhR-milH*	skim milk
die Sahne	*dee zah-nuh*	cream
die saure Sahne	*dee zou-Ruh zah-nuh*	sour cream
die Schlagsahne	*dee shlAk-zah-nuh*	whip cream
die Vollmilch	*dee fol-milH*	whole milk

Achtung!

In English, you say, "I want a slice of cheese." In German, you simply say, "I want a slice cheese," or "Ich möchte eine Scheibe Käse (*iH möH-tuh ay-nuh shay-buh käh-zuh*)." If you want to get specific about the cheese you want, however, you say, (pointing at the cheese you want), "Ich möchte eine Scheibe von diesem Käse dort (*iH möH-tuh ay-nuh shay-buh fon dee-zuhm käh-zuh doRt*)," or, "I want a slice of that cheese there."

Table 11.7 At the Bakery and Pastry Shop

German	Pronunciation	English
das Brot	*dAs bRoht*	bread
das Brötchen	*dAs bRöht-Huhn*	roll

continues

Table 11.7 Continued

German	Pronunciation	English
das Plätzchen	*dAs pläts-Huhn*	cookie
das Roggenbrot	*dAs Ro-guhn-bRoht*	rye bread
das Toastbrot	*dAs tohst-bRoht*	white bread (toast)
das Vollkornbrot	*dAs fol-koRn-bRoht*	whole-grain bread
das Weißbrot	*dAs vays-bRoht*	white bread
der Apfelstrudel	*deyR Ap-fuhl-shtRew-duhl*	apple strudel
der Berliner	*deyR beR-lee-nuhR*	jam doughnut
der Kuchen	*deyR kew-CHuhn*	cake
die Schwarzwälder	*dee shvARts-välduhR*	Black Forest (cake)
die Torte	*dee toR-tuh*	tart
Kirschtorte	*kiRsh-toR-tuh*	cherry pie

Table 11.8 At the Supermarket

German	Pronunciation	English
die Getränke	*dee guh-tRän-kuh*	drinks
das Bier	*dAs beeR*	beer
das Mineralwasser	*dAs mee-nuh-Rahl-vA-suhR*	mineral water
der Saft	*deyR zAft*	juice
die Limonade	*dee lee-moh-nah-duh*	soft drink
kohlensäurehaltig	*koh-len-zoy-Re-hAl-tiH*	carbonated
nicht kohlensäurehaltig	*niHt koh-len-zoy-Re-hAl-tiH*	non-carbonated

Wine Words

On wine labels in Germany, you will come across four different categories of grapes used for wines: *Spätlese* (*shpät-ley-suh*), indicating a dry wine, *Auslese* (*ous-ley-suh*), indicating a fairly dry wine made from ripe grapes, *Beerenauslese* (*beyR-uhn-ous-ley-suh*), indicating a sweet wine made from a special kind of very ripe grape, and *Trockenbeerenauslese* (*tRo-kuhn-bey-Ruhn-ous-ley-suh*), indicating a very sweet (usually quite expensive) wine. Here are some terms you should familiarize yourself with if you're a wine lover:

German	Pronunciation	English
(sehr) trocken	*(seyR) tRo-kuhn*	(very) dry
süß	*zühs*	sweet
etwas süß	*et-vAs zühs*	rather sweet
leicht	*layHt*	light

Here are a few terms and phrases that might help you in a German *Kneipe* (*knay-puh*, f.) or pub:

German	Pronunciation	English
ein Altbier	*ayn Alt-beeR*	a bitter ale
ein Bier vom Faß	*ayn beeR fom fAs*	a draft beer
ein dunkles Bier	*ayn doon-kluhs beeR*	a dark beer
Ein Glas Bier, bitte.	*ayn glAs beeR, bi-tuh*	A glass of beer, please.
ein helles Bier	*ayn he-luhs beeR*	a light beer
ein Pils	*ayn pilts*	a bitter (light beer)
eine Berliner Weiße mit Schuß	*ay-nuh BeR-li-nuhR vay-suh mit shoos*	a Weißbier with a dash of raspberry juice

You can use the verb *trinken* to help you order a beer or that special glass of wine.

Table 11.9 Conjugation of the Verb trinken

Person	Singular	English	Plural	English
First	ich trinke *iH tRin-kuh*	I drink	wir trinken *veeR tRin-kuhn*	we drink
Second	du trinkst *dew tRinkst*	you drink	ihr trinkt *eeR tRinkt*	you drink
(Formal)	Sie trinken *zee tRin-kuhn*		Sie trinken *zee tRin-kuhn*	
Third	er, sie, es trinken *eR, zee, es tRin-kuhn*	he, she, it drinks	sie trinken *zee tRin-kuhn*	they drink

Going Out to Eat

Germany is a country well-known for hearty, satisfying repasts. The meal you choose depends on the following factors: the kind of food you want, the kind of service you want, and your budget. Are you looking for breakfast, *das Frühstück* (*dAs fRüh-shtük*), for lunch, *das Mittagessen* (*dAs mi-tahk-e-suhn*), or for dinner, *das Abendessen* (*dAs ah-buhnt-e-suhn*)? Try one of these:

➤ der Schnellimbiss (*deyR shnel-im-bis*), fast-food restaurant

➤ das Cafe (*dAs kA-fey*), coffee house

➤ das Selbstbedienungsrestaurant (*dAs zelpst-buh-dee-nooks-Res-tou-Rohn*), cafeteria

➤ die Imbissbude (*dee im-bis-bew-duh*), snack stand

➤ der Nachtklub (*deyR nACHt-kloop*), night club

➤ das Gasthaus (*dAs gAst-hous*), tavern or inn

➤ die Kneipe (*dee knay-puh*), bar

Making Reservations

The following list contains some phrases you may find useful when dining out:

German	Pronunciation	English
Ich möchte einen Tisch reservieren.	*iH mö-Htuh ay-nuhn tish Rey-zuhR-vee-Ruhn*	I would like to reserve a table.
für heute Abend	*führ hoy-tuh ah-bent*	for this evening
für morgen Abend	*führ moR-guhn ah-bent*	for tomorrow evening
für Samstag Abend	*führ zAms-tahk ah-bent*	for Saturday night
für zwei Personen	*führ tsvay peR-zoh-nuhn*	for two people
um halb neun	*oom hAlp noyn*	at 8:30
auf der Terrasse, bitte	*ouf deyR te-RA-suh, bi-tuh*	on the terrace, please
am Fenster	*Am fen-stuhR*	at the window
im Raucherbereich	*im Rou-CHuhR-buh-RayH*	in the smoking section
im Nicht-Raucherbereich	*im niHt-Rou-HuhR-buh-RayH*	in the nonsmoking section
an der Theke	*An deyR tey-kuh*	at the bar

Remember that when you use one of these prepositional phrases in a sentence, *reservieren*—the second verb in a modal construction—should come at the end of the sentence, as in:

Ich möchte einen Tisch für heute Abend reservieren.
iH mö-Htuh ay-nuhn tish führ hoy-tuh ah-bent Rey-zuhR-vee-Ruhn
I'd like to reserve a table for this evening.

At the Restaurant

It's Saturday night, and you want to try the fare at one of the fanciest restaurants in Berlin. Call up and make a reservation by the window in the nonsmoking section. The person on the other end of the line may ask you this question:

Einen Tisch für wieviele Personen?
ay-nuhn tish fühR vee-fee-luh peR-zoh-nuhn
A table for how many?

Answer him this way:

Einen Tisch für vier Personen, bitte.
ay-nuhn tish fühR feeR peR-zoh-nuhn, bi-tuh
A table for four, please.

The terms in Table 11.10 should be of use to you when you are in a restaurant.

Table 11.10 A Table Setting

German	Pronunciation	English
das Besteck	*dAs be-stek*	cutlery
das Geschirr	*dAs guh-sheeR*	crockery
das Messer	*dAs me-suhR*	knife
der Eßlöffel	*deyR es-lö-fuhl*	soup spoon
die Kellnerin	*dee kel-nuh-Rin*	waitress
der Kellner	*deyR kel-nuhR*	waiter
der Salzstreuer	*deyR zAlts-shtRoy-uhR*	salt shaker
der Suppenteller	*deyR zoo-puhn-te-luhR*	soup dish
der Teelöffel	*deyR tey-lö-fuhl*	teaspoon
der Teller	*deyR te-luhR*	dinner plate
die Gabel	*dee gah-buhl*	fork
die Pfeffermühle	*dee pfe-fuhR-müh-luh*	pepper mill
die Serviette	*dee zeR-vee-e-tuh*	napkin

German	Pronunciation	English
die Speisekarte	*dee shpay-zuh-kAR-tuh*	menu
die Tasse	*dee tA-suh*	cup
die Tischdecke	*dee tish-de-kuh*	tablecloth
die Untertasse	*dee oon-teR-tA-suh*	saucer

I Need Another Fork, Please

If there is something missing from your table setting and you need to ask the waiter or busboy for it, the verb *brauchen* (*bRou-CHuhn*) will be the one that will get you what you want quickest. Familiarize yourself with its conjugation in Table 11.11.

Table 11.11   Conjugation of the Verb brauchen

Person	Singular	English	Plural	English
First	ich brauche *iH bRou-CHuh*	I need	wir brauchen *veeR bRou-CHuhn*	we need
Second	du brauchst *dew bRouCHst*	you need	ihr braucht *eeR bRouCHt*	you need
(Formal)	Sie brauchen *zee bRou-CHuhn*		Sie brauchen *zee bRou-CHuhn*	
Third	er, sie, es braucht *eR, zee,* *es bRouCHt*	he, she, it needs	sie brauchen *zee bRou-CHuhn*	they need

I'll Take the Cabbage Soup, Please

If you want a waiter, you can shout *Herr Ober* (*heR oh-buhR*) and there he'll be. To tell the waiter that you would like to start with an aperitif, for example, you would say: *Ich hätte gern einen Aperitif, bitte.*

Table 11.12   Soups (*die Suppen, dee zoo-puhn*)

German	Pronunciation	English
die Bauernsuppe	*dee bou-eRn-zoo-puh*	cabbage and sausage soup
die Bohnensuppe	*dee boh-nuhn-zoo-puh*	bean soup
die Frühlingssuppe	*dee fRüh-links-zsoo-puh*	spring vegetable soup
die Kraftbrühe mit Ei	*dee kRAft-bRüh-huh mit ay*	beef broth with raw egg
die Linsensuppe	*dee lin-zuhn-zoo-puh*	lentil soup
die Ochsenschanzsuppe	*dee ox-zuhn-shvAnts-zoo-puh*	oxtail soup
die Tomatensuppe	*dee toh-mah-tuhn-zoo-puh*	tomato soup

Table 11.13   Meats (*das Fleisch, dAs flaysh*)

German	Pronunciation	English
das Bündnerfleisch	*dAs bünt-nuhR-flaysh*	thinly sliced, air-dried beef
das Gulasch	*dAs goo-lAsh*	beef stew with spicy paprika
das Lammkotelett	*dAs lAm-kot-let*	lamb chop
das Schweinskotlett	*dAs shvayns-kot-let*	pork chop
der Bauernschmaus	*deyR bou-eRn-shmous*	smoked pork, sausages, dumpling, tomato, and sauerkraut
der Hackbraten	*deyR hAk-bRah-tuhn*	meatloaf
der Kalbsbraten	*deyR kAlps-bRah-tuhn*	roast veal

Made to Order

With certain dishes, you have a choice about how they're served or cooked. For example, if you order eggs, you'll want to let the waiter know how you like your eggs cooked. Your waiter may ask you something like this:

Wie wollen (möchten) Sie sie (ihn, es)?
vee vo-luhn (möH-tuhn) zee zee (een, es)
How do you want them (it)?

The adjectives in Table 11.14 give you ways to answer.

Table 11.14   How Would You Like It Prepared?

German	Pronunciation	English
angebräunt	*An-guh-bRoynt*	browned
blutig	*blew-tiH*	rare
durchgekocht	*dewRch-guh-koHt*	well-done
gedünstet	*guh-düns-tuht*	steamed
paniert	*pah-neeRt*	breaded
püriert	*püh-ReeRt*	pureed
das Omelett	*dAs om-let*	omelette
das Spiegelei	*dAs shpee-guhl-ay*	fried egg
die Rühreier	*dee RühR-ay-uhR*	scrambled eggs
hartgekocht	*hARt-guh-koCHt*	hard-boiled
pochiert	*po-sheeRt*	poached
weichgekocht	*vayH-guh-koCHt*	soft-boiled

We're All Special

Be prepared to use the following phrases to get things *your* way.

German	Pronunciation	English
Ich bin auf (einer) Diet.	*iH bin auf (ay-nuhR) dee-eyt*	I am on a diet.
Ich bin (ein) Vegetarier.	*iH bin (ayn) vey-gey-tah-Ree-uhR*	I'm a vegetarian.

continues

continued

German	Pronunciation	English
Ich kann nichts essen, was…enthält.	*iH kAn niHst e-suhn, vAs…ent-hält*	I can't eat anything with…in it.
Ich kann kein (e, -en)… essen (trinken).	*iH kAn kayn (uh, -uhn)… e-suhn (tRin-khn)*	I can't have…
die Meeresfrüchte	*dee mey-Ruhs-fRüH-tuh*	seafood
die gesättigten Fette	*dee guh-zä-tiH-tuhn fe-tuh*	saturated fats
Ich suche nach einem Gericht mit…	*iH zew-CHuh nACH ay-nuhm guh-RiHt mit*	I'm looking for a dish (that is)…
niedrigem Cholesteringehalt	*nee-dRee-guhm ko-les-tey-Reen-guh-hAlt*	low in cholesterol
niedriger Fettgehalt	*nee-dRee-guhR fet-guh-hAlt*	low in fat
niedriger Natriumgehalt	*nee-dRee-guhR nA-tRee-oom-guh-hAlt*	low in sodium
keine Milchprodukte	*kayn milH-pRo-dukt*	non-dairy
salzfrei	*zAlts-fRay*	salt-free
zuckerfrei	*tsoo-kuhR-fRay*	sugar-free

Oops!

When you want to send something back, you should be prepared to explain to your waiter what the problem is with your food.

Table 11.15 Possible Problems

German	Pronunciation	English
…ist kalt	*ist kAlt*	…is cold
…ist zu blutig	*ist tsew blew-tiH*	…is too rare
…ist übergar	*ist üh-buhR-gahR*	…is overdone

German	Pronunciation	English
…ist zäh	*ist tsäh*	…is tough
…ist angebrannt	*ist An-guh-bRAnt*	…is burned
…ist zu salzig	*ist tsew zAl-tsiH*	…is too salty
…ist zu süß	*ist tsew zühs*	…is too sweet
…ist zu scharf	*ist tsew shARf*	…is too spicy
…ist verdorben	*ist veR-doR-buhn*	…is spoiled

How to Order Your Strudel

Do you have a sweet tooth? Cake is normally eaten around four o'clock in the afternoon for *Kaffee* (*kA-fey*), an early afternoon coffee break. Table 11.16 lists some of the most common desserts.

Table 11.16   Delectable Desserts

German	Pronunciation	English
der Apfelstrudel	*deyR ap-fuhl-shtrew-duhl*	apple strudel
der Kuchen	*deyR kew-CHuhn*	cake
der Obstsalat	*deyR opst-zah-laht*	fruit salad
der Pfirsich Melba	*deyR pfeeR-ziH mel-bah*	peach Melba
der Schokoladenpudding	*deyR shoh-koh-lah-duhn-poo-ding*	chocolate pudding
die Pfannkuchen	*dee pfAn-kew-CHuhn*	crepes (pl.)
die Rote Grütze	*dee Roh-tuh gRü-tsuh*	berry pudding
die Sachertorte	*dee zA-CHuhR-toR-tuh*	chocolate cake

If you're an ice cream lover, the following terms will help you get the amount and flavor you want:

German	Pronunciation	English
das Eis	*dAs ays*	ice cream
das Erdbeereis	*dAs eRt-beyR-ays*	strawberry ice cream
das Schokoladeneis	*dAs shoh-koh-lah-den-ays*	chocolate ice cream
das Vanilleeis	*dAs vah-ni-lee-uh-ays*	vanilla ice cream
der Eisbecher	*deyR ays-be-HuhR*	dish of ice cream
mit Schlagsahne	*mit shlAk-zah-nuh*	with whipped cream
mit Schokoladensoβe	*mit shoh-koh-lah-den-zoh-suh*	with chocolate sauce

You Can Take It With You

German portions traditionally are large. If you hate waste, ask the waiter to pack what's left on your plate: *Können Sie den Rest einpacken, bitte?* (*kö-nuhn zee deyn Rest ayn-pA-kuhn, bi-tuh*). Other options? Split a dish with your dinner mate. When you want some and not all, use the phrases *ein biβchen* (*ayn bis-Huhn*), *etwas* (*et-vAs*), or *ein wenig* (*ayn vey-nik*).

Thanks! Check, Please?

Don't keep your satisfaction to yourself when you like what you've eaten. To express joy, pleasure, amazement, and wonder when a meal has been exceptional, use the following superlative phrases.

Das Essen war ausgezeichnet!
dAs e-suhn vahR ous-guh-tsayH-nuht
The meal was great!

Die Bedienung ist groβartig!
dee buh-dee-nung ist gRohs-AR-tiH
The service is great!

The very last thing you will need to know is how to ask the waiter for your bill:

Die Rechnung bitte.
dee ReH-noong bi-tuh
The check please.

Sagen Sie mal...

In most German restaurants, *das Trinkgeld* (*tRink-gelt*)—the tip—is included in the price of the meal (generally 15 percent). Still, it is common practice to "round up" the bill. If your bill is DM 10,50, for example, you might give the waiter 12 or 13 marks, and say, "Es stimmt so," the equivalent of "Keep the change."

Chapter 12

Getting It Right, When Things Go Wrong

In This Chapter

➤ Personal services

➤ Problems and solutions

➤ Comparing and contrasting

➤ Adverbs can help

You've been eating, buying things, watching TV—having, to put it mildly, a good old time. And then, all of a sudden, the problems start. Don't worry. Everything you need is just a few blocks—or perhaps even just a phone call—away. By the end of this chapter, all your problems will be taken care of.

Help for a Bad Hair Day

Is your perm coming out? Are your roots showing? Maybe you just want to return to your native land with a new do.

Whatever your reasons for wanting to venture into a hair salon, you will need to have the basic vocabulary to get your hair styled just so.

In Germany, *der Friseur-Salon* (*deyR fRee-zöhR-zah-lon*), or hairdresser, is generally for both men and women. When a woman goes to get her hair done, she says, *Ich gehe zum Friseur* (*iH gey-huh tsoom fRee-zöhR*). If you want special services such as pedicures, manicures, or facials, you would go to a beauty salon: *Ich gehe zum Kosmetiksalon* (*iH gey-huh tsoom kos-mey-tik-sah-lohn*).

To get what you want, begin your requests to the beauty consultant with the following phrase:

> Ich hätte gern…
> *iH hä-tuh geRn*
> I would like…

Table 12.1   Hair Care

German	Pronunciation	English
eine Tönung	*ay-nuh töh-noong*	a tint
ein Haarschnitt (m.)	*ayn hahR-shnit*	a haircut
eine Dauerwelle (f.)	*ay-nuh dou-uhR-ve-luh*	a perm
eine Färbung (f.)	*ay-nuh fäR-boong*	a coloring
eine Pediküre (f.)	*ay-nuh pey-dee-küh-Ruh*	a pedicure
eine Gesichtsmassage (f.)	*ay-nuh guh-ziHts-mA-sah-juh*	a facial
eine Haarwäsche (f.)	*ay-nuh hahR-vä-shuh*	a shampoo
eine Maniküre (f.)	*ay-nuh mA-nee-küh-Ruh*	a manicure

The article following the phrase *ich hätte gern* should be in the accusative case. To let someone know you'd like a haircut, say:

> Ich hätte gern einen Haarschnitt.
> *iH hä-tuh geRn ay-nuhn hahR-shnit*
> I'd like a haircut.

Another way of getting services in a beauty salon is by using the subjunctive tense of the verb *können*.

> Könnten Sie mir bitte den Pony zurechtschneiden?
> *kön-tuhn zee meeR bi-tuh deyn po-nee tsew-ReHt-shnay-duhn*
> Could you please cut my bangs?

> Könnten Sie mir bitte die Haare glätten?
> *kön-tuhn zee meeR bi-tuh dee hah-Ruh glü-tuhn*
> Could you please straighten my hair?

> Könnten Sie mir bitte die Haare fönen?
> *kön-tuhn zee meeR bi-tuh dee hah-Ruh föh-nuhn*
> Could you please blow-dry my hair?

Table 12.2 Hairstyles

German	Pronunciation	English
lang	*lAng*	long
mittellang	*mi-tuhl-lAng*	medium length
kurz	*kooRs*	short
gewellt	*guh-velt*	wavy
lockig	*lo-kiH*	curly
glatt	*glAt*	straight
stufig	*shtew-fiH*	layered
geflochten	*guh-floCH-tuhn*	braided
schwarz	*shvARts*	black
kastanienbraun	*kAs-tah-nee-uhn-bRoun*	auburn
rot	*Roht*	red
in einer dunkleren Farbe	*in ay-nuhR doonk-luh-Ruhn fAR-buh*	in a darker color
in einer helleren Farbe	*in ay-nuh he-luh-Ruhn fAR-buh*	in a lighter color
in der gleichen Farbe	*in deyR glay-Huhn fAR-buh*	in the same color

There may be certain beauty products, chemicals, or lotions that you're allergic to. Or perhaps you can't abide certain smells. If you don't like certain hair care products, speak up. Begin your request to the hairdresser with either of the following phrases:

Ich möchte kein(-e, -en)...
iH möH-tuh kayn(-uh, -uhn)
I don't want any...

Bitte, benutzen Sie kein(-e, -en)...
bi-tuh, buh-noot-tsuhn zee kayn(-uh, -uhn)
Please, don't use...

German	Pronunciation	English
das Haargel	*dAs hahR-geyl*	gel
das Haarspray	*dAs hahR-spRay*	hair spray
das Shampoo	*dAs shAm-pew*	shampoo
der Haarschaum	*deyR hahR-shoum*	mousse
die Haarlotion	*dee hahR-loh-tseeohn*	lotion
die Pflegespülung	*dee pfley-guh-shpüh-loonk*	conditioner

When You Need Help

There will undoubtedly be times, particularly if you take what you've learned of the German language and venture into a German-speaking country, when you will find yourself in need of a helping hand. The problem is, how do you get this helping hand to help you? The sections that follow will help you prepare yourself for those situations you are bound to encounter at the dry cleaners, at the Laundromat, at the shoemaker, and so on.

Words for the Wise

When you have minor problems—a stain, a broken shoe-lace, a ripped contact lens—which occur in a universe where chaos seems to dispel what little order there is, you will find the following phrases useful.

Um wieviel Uhr öffnen Sie?
oom vee-feel ewR öf-nuhn zee
What time do you open?

Um wieviel Uhr schlieben Sie?
oom vee-feel ewR shlee-suhn zee
At what time do you close?

An welchen Tagen haben Sie geöffnet (geschlossen)?
An vel-Huhn tah-guhn hah-buhn zee guh-öf-net (guh-shlo-suhn)
What days are you open (closed)?

Können Sie mein(-e, -en)...reparieren?
kö-nuh zee mayn(-uh, -uhn)...Re-pah-Ree-Ruhn
Can you fix my...for me?

Können Sie ihn (es, sie) heute reparieren?
kö-nuh zee een (es, zee) hoy-tuh Re-pah-Ree-Ruhn
Can you fix it (them) today?

Kann ich bitte eine Quittung bekommen?
kAn iH bi-tuh ay-nuh kvi-toong buh-ko-muhn
Can I have a receipt, please?

Dry Cleaning Your Dirty Laundry

Need a dry cleaner or tailor? The person helping you will probably ask you something like, "Wo liegt das Problem (*vo leekt dAs pRo-blem*)?" Knowing how to explain your problem and ask for the necessary type of service is crucial.

Das Hemd ist schmutzig.
dAs hempt ist shmoot-sik
The shirt is dirty.

Mir fehlt ein Knopf.
meeR feylt ayn knopf
I'm missing a button.

Ich habe eine Loch in meiner Hose.
iH hah-buh ay-nuh loH in may-nuhR hoh-zuh
I have a hole in my pants.

Da ist ein Flecken.
dA ist ayn fle-kuhn
There's a stain.

You've explained the problem. Now you must be clear
about what you want done to correct it. Try these phrases:

Können Sie diese(-s, -n)...für mich reinigen, bitte?
kö-nuh zee dee-suh(-s, -n)...führ miH ray-ni-guhn, bi-tuh
Can you clean this (these) for me, please?

Können Sie diese(-s, -n)...für mich bügeln, bitte?
kö-nuh zee dee-suh(-s, -n)...führ miH büh-guhln, bi-tuh
Can you iron this (these) for me, please?

Können Sie diese(-s, -n)...für mich stärken, bitte?
kö-nuh zee dee-suh(-s, -n)...führ miH shtäR-kuhn, bi-tuh
Can you starch this (these) for me, please?

Können Sie diese(-s, -n)...für mich nähen bitte?
kö-nuh zee dee-suh(-s, -n)...führ miH näh-huhn, bi-tuh
Can you sew this (these) for me, please?

Doing Your Own Laundry

Need a Laundromat? These phrases will be of use to you
in your search:

Ich suche einen Waschsalon.
iH zew-Huh ay-nuhn vash-sah-lohn
I'm looking for a laundromat.

Ich habe viel dreckige Wäsche.
iH hah-buh feel dRe-ki-guh vä-shuh
I have a lot of dirty clothes.

Ich möchte meine Wäsche waschen lassen.
iH möH-tuh may-nuh vä-shuh vA-shuhn lA-suhn
I want to have my clothes washed.

Welche Waschmaschine kann ich benutzen?
vel-Huh vAsh-mA-shee-nuh kAn iH buh-noo-tsuhn
Which washing machine can I use?

Welcher Trockner ist frei?
vel-HuhR tRok-nuhR ist fRay
Which dryer is free to use?

Wo kann ich Waschpulver kaufen?
vo kAn iH vAsh-pool-vuhR kou-fuhn
Where can I buy laundry soap?

Getting Well-Heeled

Have you been walking so much that you have worn the soles of your shoes away, the way the princess does in the fairy tale by the *Gebrüder Grimm*? Perhaps you simply want to be able to see your smiling face reflected in your polished patent leather dress shoes as you bend down to pick up a lucky *pfennig* from the sidewalk. Whatever your reasons for visiting your local shoemaker, the following phrases will help you make your desires clear.

Können Sie...für mich reparieren?
kö-nuhn zee...fühR miH rey-pah-ree-Ruhn
Can you fix...for me?

German	Pronunciation	English
diese Schuhe	*dee-suh shew-huh*	these shoes
diese Stiefel	*dee-suh shtee-fuhl*	these boots
diesen Absatz	*dee-suhn ap-zats*	this heel
diese Sohle	*dee-suh zoh-luh*	this sole

Haben Sie Schnürsenkel?
hah-buhn zee shnüR-zen-kuhl
Do you have shoe laces?

Können Sie meine Schuhe putzen, bitte?
kö-nuhn zee may-nuh shew-huh poot-zuhn, bi-tuh
Can you polish my shoes, please?

Seeing the Eye Doctor

If you happen to sit on your glasses while in Deutschland, these phrases may come in handy:

Können Sie diese Brille reparieren, bitte?
Kö-nuhn zee dee-zuh bRi-luh Rey-pah-Ree-Ruhn, bi-tuh
Can you repair these glasses for me, please?

Das Glass (das Gestell) ist zerbrochen.
dAs glAs (dAs guh-shtel) ist tseR-bRo-CHuhn
The lens (the frame) is broken.

Können Sie diese Kontaktlinsen ersetzen.
kö-nuhn zee dee-zuh kon-tAkt-lin-zuh eR-ze-tsuhn
Can you replace these contact lenses?

Verkaufen Sie Sonnenbrillen?
feR-kou-fuhn zee zo-nuhn-bRi-luhn
Do you sell sunglasses?

A Quick Course in Jewelry Repair

Has your watch stopped? If you want to catch your train and plane on time, you may want to have your watch repaired. Try these phrases when you're at the jewelers:

Meine Armbanduhr ist kaputt.
may-nuh ARm-bAnt-ewR ist kA-poot
My watch is broken.

Können Sie diese Armbanduhr reparieren?
kö-nuhn zee dee-zuh ARm-bAnt-ewR Re-pah-Ree-Ruhn
Can you repair this watch?

Meine Armbanduhr lauft zu schnell (langsam).
may-nuh ARm-bAnt-ewR loyft tsew shnel (lAng-sAm)
My watch is fast (slow).

Verkaufen Sie Batterien?
feR-kou-fuhn zee bah-tuh-Ree-uhn
Do you sell batteries?

Camera Catch Phrases

If you lost or forgot your camera, or if you simply need to buy some film, you will probably want to pay a visit to a camera shop. Here are some phrases that may come in handy:

Ich brauche einen Fotoaparat.
iH bRou-Huh ayn foh-toh-ah-pah-Raht
I need a camera.

Ich brauche eine Videokamera.
iH bRou-Huh ayn vee-dee-oh-kah-muhR-ah
I need a video camera.

Haben Sie Farbfilme (Schwarzwei[gb]film) mit 20 (36) Photos?
hah-buhn zee fARp-fil-muh (shvARts-vays-film) mit 20 (36) foh-tos
Do you have color (black-and-white) film with 20 (36) exposures?

Können Sie diesen Film entwickeln, bitte?
kö-nuhn zee dee-zuhn film ent-vi-kuhln, bi-tuh
Can you develop this film, please?

When You Need to Replace Your Passport

Here are a few common angst-inducing situations you should be prepared for and the phrases you will need to get through them.

Wo ist...?
vo ist
Where is...?

German	Pronunciation	English
das Polizeiamt	*dAs poh-li-tsay-Amt*	the police station
das amerikanische Konsulat	*dAs ah-mey-Ree-kah-ni-shuh kon-zew-laht*	the American Consulate
die amerikanische Botschaft	*dee ah-mey-Ree-kah-ni-shuh bot-shAft*	the American Embassy

Ich habe...verloren
iH hah-buh...feR-loh-Ruhn
I have lost...

German	Pronunciation	English
meinen Paß (m.)	*may-nuhn pAs*	my passport
mein Portemonaie (n.)	*mayn poRt-moh-ney*	my wallet
meine Handtasche (f.)	*may-nuh hAnt-tA-shuh*	my purse

Helfen Sie mir, bitte.
hel-fuhn zee meeR, bi-tuh
Help me, please.

Ich brauche einen Dolmetcher.
iH bRou-Huh ay-nuhn dol-met-HuhR
I need an interpreter.

Spricht jemand hier Englisch?
shpRiHt yeh-mAnt heeR eng-lish
Does anyone here speak English?

Achtung!

Just because you're in a foreign country doesn't mean you shouldn't shop around. Whether it's a hotel, a jewelry store, a clothing store, or a train station, ask about prices. Then go to the competition and ask about *their* prices. Find out who offers the best deal, and (a person would be an idiot not to) take it!

Was haben Sie gesagt?

Positive Form The form in which adverbs or adjectives appear normally, before they have taken any endings.

Comparative Form The "more" form adjectives and adverbs take when compared.

Superlative Form The "most" form adjectives and adverbs take when they are compared.

Pricing the Competition

When you're explaining to someone why you bought this here and that there, you will have to know how to use adjectives and adverbs to compare things. Adverbs and adjectives have three forms—the base form, *billig* (*bi-liH*, cheap), the comparative, *billiger* (*bi-li-guhR*, cheaper), and the superlative form *der/die/das billigste* (*deyR/dee/dAs bi-lik-stuh*) or *am billigsten* (*Am bi-lik-stuhn*) all of which mean "the cheapest." The form of the definite article and the ending on the adjective will vary according to case and gender.

Adverbs and Adjectives Compared

Adjectives and adverbs are compared by adding *-er* in English to form the comparative and by adding *-est* to form the superlative. It's quite similar in German: the ending *-er* also is used to form the comparative for both adjectives and adverbs, and *-(e)st* to form the superlative. Notice that when the comparison of an adjective is used in a sentence, the superlative ending for that adjectives is *-(e)ste*. For adverbs, the superlative ending becomes *-(e)sten.*

The following list gives you the adjective *stark* (*shtARk,* or strong) in the base, comparative, and superlative form:

Adjective Type	German	Pronunciation	English
Positive	Beate ist stark.	*bey-ah-tuh ist shtARk*	Beate is strong.
Comparative	Beate ist stärker als Peter.	*bey-ah-tuh ist shtäR-kuhR Als Pey-tuhR*	Beate is stronger than Peter.
Superlative	Maurice ist der stärkste.	*moh-Rees ist deyR shtäRk-stuh*	Maurice is the strongest.

The following list gives you the adverb *stark* in the base, comparative, and superlative form:

Adverb Type	German	Pronunciation	English
Positive	Es regnet stark.	*es Reyk-net shtARk*	It rains hard.
Comparative	Es regnet stärker.	*es Reyk-net shtäR-kuhR*	It rains harder.

Adverb Type	German	Pronunciation	English
Superlative	Es regnet am stärksten.	*es Reyk-net Am shtäRk-stuhn*	It rains the hardest.

Sagen Sie mal...

The optional (e) is used to form the superlative for adjectives whose positive form ends in -d, -s, -st, -ß, -t, -tz, or -z.

Table 12.3 lists the adjectives you will need (in their comparative and superlative forms) to be a good comparison shopper.

Table 12.3 Adjectives Used to Compare

Positive	English	Comparative	Superlative
billig *bi-liH*	cheap	billiger *bi-li-guhR*	am billigsten *Am bi-lik-stuhn*
schön *shühn*	beautiful	schöner *shöh-nuhR*	am schönsten *Am shöhn-stuhn*
groß *gRos*	big	größer *gRöh-suhR*	am größten *Am gRös-tuhn*
klein *klayn*	small	kleiner *klay-nuhR*	am kleinsten *Am klayn-stuhn*
bunt *boont*	colorful	bunter *boon-tuhR*	am buntesten *Am boon-tes-tuhn*
weich *vayH*	soft	weicher *vay-HuhR*	am weichesten *Am vay-Hes-tuhn*

continues

Table 12.3   Continued

Positive	English	Comparative	Superlative
warm *vARm*	warm	wärmer *väR-muhR*	am wäRm-stuhn *Am väRm-stuhn*
teuer *toy-uhR*	expensive	teuerer *toy-uhR-uhR*	am teuersten *Am toy-uhR-stuhn*

Remember, when forming the comparative with adverbs, add the ending *-er* to the positive form of the adverb. To form the superlative, use the formula *am* + positive form of adverb + the ending *-(e)sten*.

And Then There Were Adverbs

Adverbs are used to modify verbs or adjectives. You can use them to describe how well, how badly, or in what way something is done, as in, "He plays the piano wonderfully," or, "I swim amazingly well." In English, adverbs are formed by adding the ending *-ly* to adjectives, resulting in words like happily, quickly, slowly, moderately, and so on.

In German, almost all adjectives can be used as adverbs. There are many words that are only adverbs, however—words such as *dort* (*doRt*), or "there," and *hier* (*heeR*), or "here." The only adverbs with endings are the ones that appear in the comparative and superlative forms. To form the comparative of adverbs, add *-er* to the adverb: *Der Abenteuerfilm ist spannender als die Dokumentation*. To form the superlative, add *am* before the superlative and *-sten* to the adverb: *Der Abenteuerfilm ist am spannendsten*.

The best way to understand the difference between adverbs and adjectives is to compare sentences using the same word, first as an adjective, and then as an adverb.

Boris Becker ist ein guter Tennisspieler. (adj.)
bo-Ris be-keR ist ayn gew-tuhR te-nis-shpee-luhR
Boris Becker is a good tennis player.

Ich kann auch gut spielen. (adv.)
iH kAn ouH gewt shpee-luhn
I can also play well.

In der Disko hört man nur laute Musik. (adj.)
in deyR dis-koh höRt mAn newR lou-tuh mew-seek
In the disco you only hear loud music.

Das Orchester spielt das Stück viel zu laut. (adv.)
dAs oR-kes-tuhR shpeelt dAs shtük feel tsew lout
The orchestra plays the piece far too loudly.

Was haben Sie gesagt?

Adverbs   Words used to modify verbs or adjectives.

The word "adverb" implies its principal function—which is to be added to, or to modify, a verb. But don't let the name fool you. Adverbs can also modify adjectives, as they do in the following sentences:

Das Frühstück war sehr gut.
dAs fRüH-shtük vAR seyR gewt
The breakfast was very good.

Seine Geschichte war höchst langweilig.
say-nuh guh-shiH-tuh vAR höCHst lAnk-vay-liH
His story was very boring.

Adverbs That Don't Do Double Duty

Although most adjectives can be used as adverbs, there are many words that can be used only as adverbs. In Table 12.4 you will find a list of these common adverbs (that do not double as adjectives).

Table 12.4 Plain Old Adverbs

German	Pronunciation	English
anschließend	*An-shlee-suhnt*	then, afterward
bald	*bAlt*	soon
da	*dA*	there
danach	*dA-nahCH*	then
dort	*doRt*	there
endlich	*ent-liH*	at last
früh	*fRüh*	early
ganz	*gAnts*	quite, entirely
gelegentlich	*gey-ley-get-liH*	occasionally
gestern	*ges-tuhRn*	yesterday
heute	*hoy-tuh*	today
hier	*heeR*	here
immer	*i-muhR*	always
jetzt	*yetst*	now
manchmal	*mAnH-mahl*	sometimes
nie	*nee*	never
noch	*noCH*	still
nur	*nuR*	only
oft	*oft*	often
plötzlich	*plöts-liH*	suddenly
sehr	*seyR*	very
seit	*sayt*	since
sofort	*soh-foRt*	immediately
spät	*shpäht*	late
zusammen	*tsew-sA-muhn*	together

Achtung!

The adverb of place *morgen* means tomorrow. *Der Morgen*, however, means "the morning." To say tomorrow morning, however, you do not say *morgen Morgen* (it is redundant); instead, modify the adverb *morgen* with the adverb *früh*: *Wir gehen morgen früh nach Hause*. (We're going to the house tomorrow morning.)

Where Do Those Adverbs Belong?

Brace yourself: You're not through with adverbs yet. Adverbs can be divided into categories. The most common categories of adverbs are time, manner, and place. *Heute* in *Sie geht heute ins Kino* (*zee geyt hoy-tuh ins kee-noh*), or, "Today she goes to the movies," uses an adverb of time; *langsam* in the sentence *Er läuft langsam* (*eR loyft lang-sahm*), or, "He runs slowly," is an adverb of manner; *Hier* in *Hier fühle ich mich wie zu Hause* (*heeR füh-luh iH miH vee tsew hou-zuh*), or, "I feel at home here," is an adverb of place. So what happens when you have a number of different adverbs in one sentence? How do you know which adverb to put where? All you have to remember is this: TeMPo. Adverbs of **time** come first. Adverbs of **manner** next. Then come adverbs of **place**.

> Er fährt heute mit dem Fahrrad dorthin. (time, place)
> *eR fähRt hoy-tuh mit deym fah-rAt doRt-hin*
> He drives there today on his bicycle.

If there are two adverbs of the same type in a sentence, the more general adverb precedes the more specific adverb:

Er fährt morgen um 8 Uhr dorthin. (general time,
specific time, place)
eR fähRt moR-guhn oom ACHt ewR doRt-hin
He drives there at eight o'clock tomorrow morning.

Irregular Comparisons

Some adjectives and adverbs have irregular comparative
and superlative forms. Yes, you guessed it: You're simply
going to have to commit these to memory.

Positive	English	Comparative	English	Superlative	English
gern *geRn*	gladly	lieber *lee-buhR*	more gladly	am liebsten *Am leep-stuhn*	most gladly
gut *gewt*	good	besser *be-suhR*	better	am besten *Am be-stuhn*	the best
hoch *hoCH*	high	höher *höh-huhR*	higher	am höchsten *Am höH-stuhn*	the highest
nah *nah*	close	näher *näh-huhR*	closer	am nächsten *Am näH-stuhn*	the closest
oft *oft*	often	öfter *öft-uhR*	more often	am öftesten *Am öf-tes-tuhn*	the most often
viel *feel*	much	mehr *meyR*	more	am meisten *Am may-stuhn*	the most

Chapter 13

Just What the Doctor Ordered

In This Chapter

➤ Symptoms, complaints, and illnesses

➤ The irregular verb *tun* in the expression *weh tun*

➤ Expressing how long

➤ How to use reflexive verbs

➤ Learning about drugstore and medical items

➤ Using the present perfect

➤ All about the helping verbs *haben* and *sein*

➤ Asking questions and giving answers in the past tense

In this chapter, you'll learn key words and phrases to complain about everything from a headache to a not-so-happy tummy. These phrases can really come in handy if you're traveling in a German-speaking place.

It's All in Your Head

The first thing you need to know is how to tell the doctor where, specifically, you're experiencing pain or discomfort. Try some of the words in Table 13.1 (some of these can also come in handy on a hot date...).

Table 13.1 Parts of the Body

German	Pronunciation	English
das Auge	*dAs ou-guh*	eye
das Bein	*dAs bayn*	leg
das Gehirn	*dAs guh-hiRn*	brain
das Gesicht	*dAs guh-ziHt*	face
das Handgelenk	*dAs hAnt-guh-lenk*	wrist
das Herz	*dAs heRts*	heart
das Knie	*dAs knee*	knee
das Ohr	*dAs ohR*	ear
der Arm	*deyR ARm*	arm
der Busen	*deyR bew-zuhn*	breast
der Finger	*deyR fin-guhR*	finger
der Fingernagel	*deyR fin-guR-ney-guhl*	fingernail
der Fuß	*deyR fews*	foot
der Fußknöchel	*deyR fews-nö-Huhl*	ankle
der Hals	*deyR hals*	neck
der Kopf	*deyR kopf*	head
der Körper	*deyR köR-puhR*	body
der Magen	*deyR mah-guhn*	stomach
der Mund	*deyR moont*	mouth
der Rücken	*deyR Rü-kuhn*	back
der Zahn	*deyR tsahn*	tooth
die Zehe	*dee tsay*	toe

German	Pronunciation	English
die Brust	*dee bRoost*	chest
die Hand	*dee hAnt*	hand
die Haut	*dee hout*	skin
die Kehle	*dee keh-luh*	throat
die Nase	*dee nah-zu*	nose
die Schulter	*dee shool-tuhR*	shoulder
die Wirbelsäule	*dee viR-buhl-zoy-luh*	spine
die Zunge	*dee tsoon-guh*	tongue
die Lippe	*dee li-puh*	lip

Telling the Doctor What She Needs to Know

When you go to the doctor, the first question will probably be, *Was haben Sie (vAs hah-buhn zee)?*, or "What's troubling you?" Use the following formula to answer:

Ich habe + body part that hurts + *-schmerzen.*

Examples:

Ich habe Bauchschmerzen.
iH hah-buh bouH-shmeR-tsuhn
I have a stomachache

Ich habe Zahnschmerzen.
iH hah-buh tsahn-shmeR-tsuhn
I have a toothache.

Ich habe Kopfschmerzen.
iH hah-buh kopf-shmeR-tsuhn
I have a headache.

Maybe your traveling companion was the one dumb enough to stay up all night drinking round after round of German beer on an empty stomach. To speak about someone else's pains, conjugate the verb *haben*:

Er hat Halsschmerzen.
eR hAt hAls-shmeR-tsuhn
He has a sore throat.

Another way of talking about your symptoms is by using the expression *weh tun* (*vey tewn*)—to hurt—which requires an indirect object pronoun. Before you learn how to use this expression, familiarize yourself with the irregular verb *tun* (*toon*), to do, found in Table 13.2.

Table 13.2   The Verb tun

Person	Singular	English	Plural	English
First	ich tue *iH tew-uh*	I do	wir tun *veeR tewn*	we do
Second	du tust *dew tewst*	you do	ihr tut *eeR tewt*	you do
(Formal)	Sie tun *zee tewn*		Sie tun *zee tewn*	
Third	er, sie, es tut *eR, zee, es tewt*	he, she, it does	sie tun *zee tewn*	they do

Was haben Sie gesagt?

You should note that the order of the words in sentences using *weh tun* can change without the meaning of the sentence being altered:

Mir tut der Fuß weh.

Der Fuß tut mir weh.

The basic formula you will need to create a sentence using the expression *weh tun* is:

Body part + conjugated form of *tun* + indirect object pronoun + *weh*.

Getting Specific

You may need to come up with something more specific than a vague ache or pain to give your doctor a shot at curing you. Consult Table 13.3 for more specific symptoms.

Table 13.3 Other Symptoms

German	Pronunciation	English
das Fieber	*dAs fee-buhR*	fever
der Schüttelfrost	*deyR shü-tuhl-fRost*	chills
der (Haut)Ausschlag	*deyR (hout)ous-shlahk*	rash
der Abseβ	*deyR Ap-ses*	abscess
der blaue Fleck	*deyR blou-uh flek*	bruise
der Durchfall	*deyR dooRCH-fAl*	diarrhea
der gebrochene Knochen	*deyR ge-bRo-Huh-nuh kno-Huhn*	broken bone
der Husten	*deyR hew-stuhn*	cough
der Knoten	*deyR knoh-tuhn*	lump
der Krampf	*deyR kRAmpf*	cramps
der Schmerz	*deyR shmeRts*	pain
die Beule	*dee boy-luh*	bump
die Blase	*dee blah-zuh*	blister
die Magenverstimmung	*dee mah-guhn-feR-shti-moonk*	indigestion

Hatten Sie jemals...?
hA-tuhn zee yey-mAls
Have you ever had...?

Haben Sie eine Krankenversicherung?
hah-buhn zee ay-nuh kRAn-kuhn-feR-zi-Huh-Roong
Do you have health insurance?

Leiden Sie unter…?
lay-duhn zee oon-tuhR
Do you suffer from…?

Have You Felt This Way Long?

Among the many questions your nurse or doctor will ask you will be, *Seit wann haben Sie diese Krankheit* (*zayt vAn hah-buhn zee dee-zuh kRAnk-hayt*)? or, "How long have you had this illness?" Your doctor may also ask you the following question: *Wie lange haben Sie diese Beschwerden schon* (*vee lAn-guh hah-buhn zee dee-zuh buh-shveR-duhn shon*)? or, "How long have you had these problems?" Answer either of these questions with the following construction:

> *Seit* + amount of time you've been sick.

Don't forget that the prepositional phrase following the preposition *seit* requires the dative case.

Example:

> Seit einer Woche.
> *zayt ay-nuhR vo-Huh.*
> For a week.

Your Illness Is Reflexive

To express how you feel, use the reflexive verb *sich fühlen*. The *sich* in front of this verb is known as a *reflexive pronoun*, because it refers back to the subject. It may help you to think of reflexive verbs and their pronouns as verbs where the action performed "reflects back" onto the subject performing the action. Table 13.4 shows you how to conjugate the reflexive verb *sich fühlen* using the correct reflexive pronouns (remember, in the infinitive form, reflexive verbs always take the reflexive pronoun *sich*).

Table 13.4   The Verb sich fühlen

English	Singular	Plural
I feel/we feel	ich fühle mich *iH füh-luh miH*	wir fühlen uns *veeR füh-luhn oonts*
you feel	du fühlst dich *dew fühlst dich*	ihr fühlt euch *eeR fühlt oyH*
(Formal)	Sie fühlen sich *zee füh-luhn ziH*	Sie fühlen sich *zee füh-luhn ziH*
he, she, it feels/they feel	er, sie, es fühlt sich *eR, zee, es fühlt ziH*	sie fühlen sich *zee füh-luhn ziH*

Flex Your Reflexive Verbs

Reflexive pronouns show that a subject is performing the action of the verb on itself. In other words, the subject and the reflexive pronoun both refer to the same person(s) or thing(s), as in the sentences, "He hurt himself," and "We enjoyed ourselves." Table 13.5 shows reflexive pronouns as they should appear with their reflexive verbs in both the dative and in the accusative.

Table 13.5   Accusative and Dative Reflexive Pronouns

Accusative Pronouns	English	Dative Pronouns	English
mich (*miH*)	myself	mir (*meeR*)	for myself
dich (*diH*)	yourself	dir (*deeR*)	for yourself
sich (*ziH*)	yourself (formal)	sich (*ziH*)	yourself (formal)
uns (*onts*)	ourselves	uns (*oonts*)	for ourselves

continues

Table 13.5 Continued

Accusative Pronouns	English	Dative Pronouns	English
euch (*oyH*)	yourselves	euch (*oyH*)	for yourselves
sich (*ziH*)	themselves	sich (*ziH*)	for themselves

Compare the pronouns used in the following sentences:

1. Sie fühlt sich schlecht.
   zee fühlt ziH shleHt
   She feels bad.

2. Du kaufst dir ein Medikament.
   dew koufst deeR ayn me-dee-kah-ment
   You buy yourself medicine.

Do you see the difference? The second person singular reflexive pronoun (it's a mouthful, we know, but there's no other way of putting it) in the first sentence appears in the accusative case. Why? Because in the first sentence, the reflexive pronoun serves as a direct object. The second person singular reflexive pronoun in the second sentence appears in the dative case. In the second sentence it serves as an indirect object.

To Reflex or Not to Reflex

Sometimes it is unclear from the English verb whether the German verb will be reflexive. For this reason it is best to familiarize yourself with common reflexive verbs in German (see Table 13.6).

Table 13.6 Common Reflexive Verbs

German	Pronunciation	English
sich waschen	*ziH vA-shuhn*	to wash (oneself)
sich setzen	*ziH ze-tsuhn*	to sit (oneself) down

German	Pronunciation	English
sich treffen	*ziH tRe-fuhn*	to meet (each other)
sich anmelden	*ziH An-mel-duhn*	to sign (oneself) up
sich anziehen	*ziH An-zee-huhn*	to dress (oneself)
sich ankleiden	*ziH An-klay-duhn*	to dress (oneself)
sich ausziehen	*ziH ous-tsee-huhn*	to undress (oneself)
sich rasieren	*ziH Rah-zee-Ruhn*	to shave (oneself)

Was haben Sie gesagt?

Reflexive Verbs Verbs that always take reflexive pronouns, because the action of the verb reflects back on the subject of the sentence.

Reflexive Pronouns Pronouns that form a part of a reflexive verb where the action refers back to the subject.

Achtung!

When reflexive verbs are used in German, the reflexive pronoun must be stated (in many cases, the reflexive pronoun can be left out in English, as in the sentence, "I shaved before going to the wedding.").

Commanding Reflexively

When you use reflexive verbs to tell your husband to shave or to tell your children to wash their hands before dinner, the reflexive pronoun usually comes at the end of the sentence, unless the reflexive verb is one with a separable prefix. Remember, when you use the formal second person singular or plural, you must always include *Sie* as part of the command:

Waschen Sie sich!
vA-shun zee ziH
Wash yourself!

Wascht euch!
vAsht oyH
Wash yourselves!

Ziehe dich an!
tsee-huh diH An
Get dressed!

At the Drugstore

You can find most of the items in Table 13.7 in either a *Drogerie*, superstore, or in one of the smaller supermarkets in Germany.

Wo kann ich ein(-e, -en)…bekommen?
vo kAn iH ayn(-uh, -uhn)…buh-ko-muhn
Where can I get…?

Table 13.7   Drugstore Items

German	Pronunciation	English
das (milde) Abführmittel	*dAs (mil-duh) Ap-führR-mi-tuhl*	laxative (mild)
das Asperin	*dAs As-pey-Reen*	aspirin
das Enthaarungswachs	*dAs ent-hah-Roonks-vAks*	depilatory wax

German	Pronunciation	English
das Heizkissen	*dAs hayts-ki-suhn*	heating pad
das Körperpuder	*dAs köR-peR-pew-duhR*	talcum powder
das Mundwasser	*dAs moont-vA-suhR*	mouthwash
der (elektrische) Rasierer	*deyR (ey-lek-tRi-shuh) Rah-zee-RuhR*	razor (electric)
der Eisbeutel	*deyR ays-boy-tuhl*	ice pack
der Erste-Hilfe-Kasten	*deyR eR-stuh-hil-fuh-kA-stuhn*	first-aid kit
der Hustensaft	*deyR hew-stuhn-sAft*	cough syrup
der Kamm	*deyR kAm*	brush
der Schnuller	*deyR shnoo-luhR*	pacifier
der Spiegel	*deyR shpee-guhl*	mirror
die Aknemedizin	*dee Ak-nuh-mey-dee-tseen*	acne medicine
die Augentropfen	*dee ou-guhn-tRo-pfuhn*	eye drops
die Enthaarungscreme cream	*dee ent-hah-rooks-kReym*	depilatory
die Feuchtigkeitscreme	*dee foyH-tiH-kayts-kreym*	moisturizer
die Flasche	*dee flA-shuh*	bottle
die Heftpflaster (n.)	*dee heft-pflA-stuhR*	Band-Aids
die Hustenbonbons (n.)	*dee hew-stuhn-bon-bons*	cough drops
die Kondome (n.)	*dee kon-doh-muh*	condoms
die Mullbinde	*dee mool-bin-duh*	gauze bandage
die Nagelfeile	*dee nah-guhl-fay-luh*	nail file
die Nasentropfen	*dee nah-zuhn-tRo-pfuhn*	nose drops
die Pinzette	*dee pin-tse-tuh*	tweezers
die Rasiercreme	*dee Rah-zeeR-kReym*	shaving cream
die Rasierklinge	*dee Rah-zeeR-klin-guh*	razor blade
die Schere	*dee shey-ruh*	scissors
die Schlaftabletten (f.)	*dee shlahf-tA-ble-tuhn*	sleeping pills

continues

Table 13.7 Continued

German	Pronunciation	English
die Sicherheitsnadeln (f.)	*dee zi-HuhR-hayts-nah-duhln*	safety pins
die Taschentücher (n.)	*dee tA-shuhn-tüh-HuhR*	tissues
die Watte	*dee vA-tuh*	cotton
die Wattestäbchen (n.)	*dee vA-tuh-shtäp-Huhn*	cotton swabs
die Windeln (f.)	*dee vin-duhln*	diapers
die Zahnbürste	*dee tsahn-büR-stuh*	toothbrush
ein (Magen) säure neutralisierendes Mittel	*ayn (mah-guhn)zoy-Ruh noy-tRah-lee-zee-Ren-duhs mi-tuhl*	an antacid

Back to the Past

We've been working in present tense so far, but as you know, there's more to life than the present. There are a number of different ways you can speak in the past tense. In English, for example, you can say, "I went to the store." In German, this is referred to as *das Präteritum* (*dAs pRä-tey-Ree-toom*), or the simple past. You also can say, "I have gone to the store." This tense is referred to as *das Perfekt* (*dAs peR-fekt*), or the present perfect tense. When you say, "I had gone to the store," you are speaking in the past in yet another way: this is referred to as *das Plusquamperfekt* (*dAs ploos-kvahm-peR-fekt*) or the past perfect tense. This chapter focuses on the formation of *das Perfekt*, the most common way of speaking in the past in German.

Verbs With Strength

You already have a head start on the formation of the perfect tense in German. English and German form the perfect tense in much the same way. Both languages use an

auxiliary or helping verb (have/*haben*) with the past participle to form the present perfect tense: I have bought/*ich
habe gekauft*. The only hitch is, some verbs in German use
the verb to be (*sein*) as an auxiliary: *Ich bin gegangen* (I
have gone). Here's the basic formula for forming the
Perfekt:

> Subject + the conjugated form of *sein* or *haben* in the
> present + past participle.

The important thing to remember is that once you learn
how to form the past participle, you won't have any
trouble speaking in the past. The past participle never
changes. Only the auxiliary verbs *haben* and *sein* change
to agree with the subject. So how is the past participle
formed? Many past participles take *ge-* at the beginning of
the verb (when you're dealing with verbs with separable
prefixes, however, the *ge-* comes after the separable prefix
in the formation of the past participle).

All strong verbs have a past participle ending in *-en*. Do
you remember strong verbs from Chapter 5? The main difference between strong and weak verbs is that strong verbs
usually have a vowel change in one of their principal
parts: third person singular, present; simple past; past participle. English verbs follow this pattern too: sing, sang,
sung (in German, *singen, sang, gesungen*). Think of strong
verbs as verbs so stubborn that they insist on having their
own way. There are patterns of vowel changes that these
verbs follow, but it would probably take you longer to
memorize these patterns than to memorize the past participle for the strong verbs you use. Our advice to you? Start
memorizing. In the following list, *hat* means that the auxiliary verb is *haben* and *ist* means that it is *sein*.

Infinitive	Third Person Sing. + Past Participle	Pronunciation	English Past Participle (have or had)
backen	hat gebacken	*hAt guh-bA-kuhn*	bake(d)
bleiben	ist geblieben	*ist guh-blee-buhn*	stay(ed)
genießen	hat genossen	*hAt guh-no-suhn*	enjoy(ed)
fahren	ist gefahren	*ist guh-fah-Ruhn*	drive (driven)
heben	hat gehoben	*hAt guh-hoh-buhn*	lift(ed), raise(ed)
tun	hat getan	*hAt guh-tahn*	do (done)
gehen	ist gegangen	*ist guh-gAn-guhn*	go (gone)
laufen	ist gelaufen	*ist guh-lou-fuhn*	run, walk(ed)
nehmen	hat genommen	*hAt guh-noh-muhn*	take (taken)

In the following sentences, two verbs from the list are used along with the conjugated auxiliary verb *haben* or *sein* to form sentences in the *Perfekt*. See if you can get a feel for how it's done:

> Sie hat ihre Schlaftabletten genommen.
> *zee hAt ee-Ruh shlAf-tAb-le-tuhn guh-no-muhn*
> She took her sleeping pills.

> Du bist zur Drogerie gegangen.
> *dew bist tsooR dRoh-guh-Ree guh-gAn-guhn*
> You have gone to the drugstore.

As you can see, to form the *Perfekt* with strong verbs, all you have to do is conjugate *haben* correctly and add *ge-* to the beginning of the strong verb in its altered past-participle form.

Verbs That Are Weak

The difference between the formation of the *Perfekt* with strong and weak verbs is that the past participles of weak verbs end in *-t*. For this reason, when you are forming a past participle, it's important to know whether the verb is weak or strong. *Gegangen* is a strong verb. It would be as incorrect to give it the weak verb ending *-t* in the past participle (resulting in the unfortunate *Ich habe gegangt*) as it would be to say "I have went" in English.

Weak verbs were discussed in Chapter 5. Weak verbs, when conjugated, follow a set pattern of rules and retain the same stem vowel throughout the conjugation. After you've come up with the past participle (you can always just look it up in a book of German verbs), just plug it into this formula:

Subject (noun or pronoun) + the conjugated form of *sein* or *haben* in the present tense + past participle.

Here are some common weak verbs and their past participles:

Infinitive	Third Person Sing. + Past Participle	Pronunciation	English Past Participle (have or had)
antworten	hat geantwortet	*hAt guh-Ant-voR-tuht*	answer(ed)
arbeiten	hat gearbeitet	*hAt guh-AR-bay-tuht*	work(ed)
gebrauchen	hat gebraucht	*hAt guh-bRouCHt*	use(ed)
trauen	hat getraucht	*hAt guh-tRouCHt*	trust(ed), marry (married)
träumen	hat geträumt	*hAt guh-tRoymt*	dream(ed)
versuchen	hat versucht	*hAt feR-sooHt*	try (tried)

Verbs That Are Mixed

You may remember mixed verbs from Chapter 5, too. They are known as "mixed" because, like a co-dependent couple, they share both strong and weak tendencies. They add the *-t* ending to form their past participle, just as weak verbs do, but—like strong verbs—the stem vowel of the infinitive changes in the past tense. Here is a list of the infinitives and past participles of some common mixed verbs:

Infinitive	Third Person Sing. + Past Participle	Pronunciation	English Past Participle (have or had)
brennen	hat gebrannt	*hAt guh-bRAnt*	burn(ed)
bringen	hat gebracht	*hAt guh-bRACHt*	bring (brought)
denken	hat gedacht	*hAt guh-dACHt*	think (thought)
kennen	hat gekannt	*hAt guh-kAnt*	know (known)
wissen	hat gewußt	*hAt guh-voost*	know (known)

Using Sein in the Perfekt

Haben is used far more frequently than *sein* in the formation of the *Perfekt*. There are, however, some commonly used verbs that use *sein* (you are already familiar with some of them). These are generally *intransitive verbs* that almost always express motion (or a change of condition). Familiarize yourself with the past participles of the most commonly used of these verbs:

Infinitive	Third Person Sing. + Past Participle	Pronunciation	English Past Participle (have or had)
sein	ist gewesen	*ist guh-vey-suhn*	be (been)
werden	ist geworden	*ist guh-voR-duhn*	become
bleiben	ist geblieben	*ist guh-bliebuhn*	stay(ed)
kommen	ist gekommen	*ist guh-ko-muhn*	come
gehen	ist gegangen	*ist guh-gAn-guhn*	go (gone)
reisen	ist gereist	*ist guh-Rayst*	travel(ed)

Don't Put Off Till Tomorrow What You Didn't Do Yesterday

As a general rule, when you say "no" in the past, *nicht* comes after the auxiliary verb *sein*. With verbs that take *haben*, *nicht* comes after the direct object. *Nicht* always precedes the past participle.

Ich bin nicht in die Drogerie gegangen.
iH bin niHt in dee dRoh-guh-Ree guh-gAn-guhn
I did not go to the drugstore.

Ich habe meine Vitamine nicht genommen.
iH hah-buh may-nuh vee-tah-mee-nuh niHt guh-no-muhn
I did not take my vitamins.

Was haben Sie gesagt?

Intransitive Verbs Verbs that do not have an object.

Transitive Verbs Verbs that have an object.

Questioning the Past

In case you're afraid that you were going to have to learn something entirely new to form questions in the past tense, don't be. To ask questions in the past tense, you can use intonation. To do this, just speak with a rising inflection.

Du hast an die Reise gedacht?
Dew hAst An dee Ray-suh gu-dACHt
Have you thought about the trip?

Another way of asking questions is by adding the word *oder* (*oh-duhR*) or the phrase *nicht wahr* (*niHt vahR*) to the end of your statements:

Du hast an die Reise gedacht, oder?
Dew hAst An dee Ray-suh gu-dACHt, oh-duhR
You have thought about the trip, right?

Du hast an die Reise gedacht, nicht wahr?
Dew hAst An dee Ray-suh gu-dACHt, niHt vahR
You have thought about the trip, haven't you?

The most common way of forming questions is by reversing the word order of the subject nouns or pronouns and the conjugated form of the verb (this is called *inversion*):

Du bist nach Hause gegangen.
Bist du nach Hause gegangen?

Chapter 14

Phone, Fax, E-mail, and Snail Mail

In This Chapter

➤ How to make phone calls, plus phone etiquette

➤ How to use reflexive verbs in the past tense

➤ Fax, e-mail, and snail mail

➤ All about the verbs *schreiben* (to write) and *lesen* (to read)

➤ Knowing the difference between *wissen* and *kennen*

This chapter teaches you how to place a local or international call from a German, Swiss, or Austrian city, and how to deal with wrong numbers and other problems you may encounter when dealing with the phone system. Along the way, you'll also learn about using reflexive verbs in the past tense.

You Just Pick Up the Phone and...

Before you even get near a phone booth, be prepared for something new. Expect the procedure you will use to make local and long-distance calls to be different from the one you're used to. The best case scenario really would be for you to find someone to walk and talk you through the procedure the first time around, but if this is impossible, read the instructions in the phone booth carefully. If you need to make an operator-assisted call, you'll have to learn to identify the type of call you're trying to make. Table 14.1 lists your options.

Table 14.1   Types of Phone Calls

German	Pronunciation	English
das Auslandsgespräch	*dAs ous-lAnts-ge-shpRähH*	out-of-the-country call
das Ferngespräch	*dAs feRn-ge-shpRähH*	long-distance call
das Ortsgespräch	*dAs oRts-ge-shpRähH*	local call
das R-Gespräch	*dAs eR-ge-shpRähH*	collect call

Your Basic German Telephone

Perhaps you're lucky enough to have a German friend explain the whole procedure of making a long-distance call to you before you even step into a phone booth. To be able to understand what she's saying, you'll have to familiarize yourself with the parts of a German phone and the other helpful words in Table 14.2.

Table 14.2   The Telephone

German	Pronunciation	English
das öffentliche Telefon	*dAs ö-fent-li-Huh tey-ley-fohn*	public phone

German	Pronunciation	English
das Telefonbuch	*dAs tey-ley-fohn-bewCH*	telephone book
das tragbare (schnurlose) Telefon	*dAs tRahk-bah-Ruh (shnooR-loh-zuh) tey-ley-fohn*	cordless phone (portable phone)
der Anrufbeantworter	*deyR An-Rewf-be-Ant-vohR-tuhR*	answering machine
der Lautsprecher	*deyR lout-shpRe-HuhR*	speaker telephone
der Münzeinwurf	*deyR münts-ayn-vewRf*	slot
der Telefonhörer	*deyR tey-ley-fohn-höh-RuhR*	receiver
die Auskunft	*dee ous-koonft*	information
die Geldrückgabetaste	*dee gelt-Rük-gah-buh-tAs-tuh*	coin return button
die Münzrückgabe	*dee münts-Rük-gah-buh*	coin return slot
die Tastatur	*dee tA-stah-tewR*	keypad
die Telefonkarte	*dee tey-ley-fohn-kAR-tuh*	phone card
die Telefonnummer	*dee tey-ley-fohn-noo-muhR*	telephone number
die Telefonzelle	*dee tey-ley-fohn-tse-luh*	booth
die Vermittlung	*dee feR-mi-tloong*	operator
die Wählscheibe	*dee vähl-shay-buh*	dial
die Wähltaste	*dee vähl-tA-stuh*	button

You're all set to place your call. If you're calling from a hotel, be prepared to pay your phone bill in blood—hotels are infamous for the exorbitant rates they charge for long-distance calls. The more economical thing to do would be to purchase a phone card (these can be purchased at a post office). The magnetic strip, similar to the strip on credit cards, will enable you to use phone booths around the city.

Achtung!

Calling overseas from hotels can be very expensive! Long-distance phone calls can be made from most phone booths in Germany, Switzerland, and Austria. Look for the sign Ausland/International near the phone.

Have Your Phone Card Ready

In Germany, there are still a few public phone booths left that accept 10 pf, 1 DM, and 5 DM coins, but the majority take only phone cards, or *Telefonkarten* (*tey-ley-fohn-kAR-tuhn*). In Germany, information for local calls is 1188; for calls in Europe dial 00118; for the German operator, dial 101; and for the long-distance operator, dial 0010. Remember, it's cheaper to make calls on weekends and after 8 p.m.

Table 14.3 Words You May Need to Make a Phone Call

German	Pronunciation	English
*an*rufen	*An-Rew-fuhn*	to call
auf ein Amtszeichen warten	*ouf ayn Amts-tsay-Huhn vAR-tuhn*	to wait for the dial tone
auflegen	*ouf-ley-guhn*	to hang up (the receiver)
den Hörer *ab*nehmen	*deyn höh-RuhR Ap-ney-muhn*	to pick up (the receiver)
die Leitung ist besetzt	*dee lay-toong ist be-zetst*	the line is busy
die Vorwahl kennen	*dee fohR-vahl ke-nuhn*	to know the area code

German	Pronunciation	English
eine Münze *ein*werfen	*ay-nuh mün-tsuh ayn-veR-fuhn*	to insert a coin
eine Nachricht *hinter*lassen	*ay-nuh nACH-RiHt hin-tuhR-lA-suhn*	to leave a message
eine Telefonkarte (f.) *ein*führen	*ay-nuh tey-ley-fohn-kAR-tuh ayn-füh-Ruhn*	to insert the card
mit der Vermittlung sprechen	*mit deyR feR-mit-loong shpRe-Huhn*	to speak to the operator
telefonieren	*tey-ley-foh-nee-Ruhn*	to telephone
wählen	*väh-luhn*	to dial
zurückrufen	*tsew-Rük-Rew-fuhn*	to call back
das Telefon klingelt	*dAs tey-ley-fon klin-guhlt*	the phone rings

The verbs with italicized prefixes are verbs with separable prefixes.

When Your Call Won't Go Through and Other Problems

There are many problems you can run into when you're making a phone call. You may dial the wrong number, there may be a never-ending busy signal, or you may continue to get the sound of a machine when it's a person you're trying to connect with. Here are some samples of phrases you may hear (or be in a position to say) when you run into rough times on the phone.

Welche Nummer haben sie gewählt?
velHuh noo-muhR hah-buhn zee guh-vählt
What number did you dial?

Es tut mir leid. Ich muß mich verwählt haben.
es toot miR layt. iH moos miH feR-vählt hah-buhn
I'm sorry. I must have dialed the wrong number.

Wir wurden unterbrochen.
veeR vooR-duhn oon-tuhR-bRo-CHuhn
We got disconnected.

Bitte wählen Sie die Nummer noch einmal.
bi-tuh väh-luhn zee dee noo-muhR noCH ayn-mahl
Please redial the number.

Diese Telefonleitung wurde abgestellt.
dee-zuh tey-ley-fohn-lay-toong vooR-duh ap-guh-shtelt
This telephone number has been disconnected.

Das Telefon ist defekt (außer Betrieb).
dAs tey-ley-fohn ist dey-fekt (ou-suhR be-tReep)
The telephone is out of order.

Rufen Sie mich später zurück.
Rew-fuhn zee miH shpäh-tuhR tsew-RüK
Call me back later.

Da ist ein Rauschen in der Leitung.
dA ist ayn Rou-shuhn in deyR lay-toong
There's static on the line.

Ich kann Sie akustisch nicht verstehen.
iH kAn zee A-koos-tish niHt feR-shtey-huhn
I can't hear you.

Er meldet sich nicht.
eR mel-det ziH niHt
He doesn't answer the phone.

Ich muß auflegen.
iH moos ouf-ley-guhn
I have to hang up.

Explaining Why You Didn't Call

Were you unable to phone someone who was expecting your call? You'll probably have to give the person a reason. To do this, you may need to use reflexive verbs in the

Präteritum. All reflexive verbs use *haben* as an auxiliary verb in the present perfect.

Ich habe mich verwählt.	Wir haben uns verwählt.
Du hast dich verwählt.	Sie haben sich verwählt.
Er/Sie/Es hat sich verwählt.	Sie haben sich verwählt.

To form the negative with reflexive verbs, *nicht* follows the reflexive pronoun.

> Er hat sich nicht gemeldet.

There are a number of ways you can form negative questions in the past with reflexive verbs:

➤ Through inversion: Hat er sich nicht gemeldet?

➤ Through intonation: Er hat sich nicht gemeldet?

➤ By using the tag *oder* or *nicht wahr*: Er hat sich nicht gemeldet, nicht wahr?

Getting Online in Germany

Faxes, modems, e-mail, and the Internet have spread their tentacles far and wide. If you need to send a fax or e-mail from Germany, you may want to familiarize yourself with the following terms:

German	Pronunciation	English
das Faxgerät	*dAs faks-guh-Rät*	fax machine
die Faxnummer	*dAs faks-noo-muhR*	fax number
ein Fax senden	*ayn faks zen-duhn*	to send a fax
etwas faxen	*et-vAs fak-suhn*	to fax something
das Fax-Modem	*dAs faks-moh-dem*	fax modem
das Internet	*dAs in-teR-net*	Internet
die E-Mail	*dee ee-meyl*	e-mail

continues

continued

German	Pronunciation	English
eine Nachricht senden	*dee nACH-RiHt zen-duhn*	to send a message
die E-Mail Adresse	*dee ee-meyl A-dRe-suh*	e-mail address

Remember Snail Mail?

Regular letters cost anywhere from 2 DM to 4 DM. But let's start with the basics. Before you do any letter or post-card writing, you're going to want to know how to ask for paper, envelopes, and other items.

Table 14.4 Mail and Post Office Terms

German	Pronunciation	English
das Paket	*dAs pah-keyt*	package, parcel
das Porto	*dAs poR-toh*	postage
das Postfach	*dAs post-fACH*	post office box
das Telegramm	*dAs tey-ley-gRAm*	telegram
der Absender	*deyR Ap-zen-duhR*	sender
der Brief	*deyR bReef*	letter
der Briefkasten	*deyR bReef-kAs-tuhn*	mailbox
der Briefumschlag	*deyR bReef-oom-shlahk*	envelope
der Empfänger	*deyR emp-fän-guhR*	addressee
der Postbeamte	*deyR post-bey-Am-tuh*	postal worker
der Telefondienst	*deyR tey-ley-fohn-deenst*	telephone service
die Briefmarke	*dee bReef-maR-kuh*	stamp
die Bundespost	*dee boon-duhs-post*	federal postal service
die Luftpost	*dee looft-post*	air letter
die Postanweisung	*dee post-An-vay-zoong*	postal order

German	Pronunciation	English
die Postkarte	*dee post-kAR-tuh*	postcard
ein Bogen (m.) Briefmarken	*ayn boh-guhn bReef-mAR-kuhn*	a sheet of stamps

Mailing Your Letter

You've written your letter, folded it, doused it with perfume, and scribbled your return address and the address of your beloved on the envelope. Now all you have to do is find a mailbox. If you don't know where one is, ask:

Wo ist das nächste Postamt?
voh ist dAs näH-stuh post-Amt
Where is the nearest post office?

Wo finde ich den nächsten Briefkasten?
voh fin-duh iH deyn näH-stuhn bReef-kA-stuhn
Where do I find the nearest mail box?

Of course, different kinds of letters and packages require different kinds of forms and have different postal rates. It's important that you know how to ask for the type of service you need:

Was kostet das Porto?
vAs kos-tuht dAs poR-toh
What's the postal rate?

German	Pronunciation	English
für das Ausland	*führ dAs ous-lAnt*	for a foreign country
für die Vereinigten Staaten	*führ dee feR-ay-nik-tuhn shtah-tuhn*	for the United States
für einen Luftpostbrief	*führ ay-nuhn looft-post-bReef*	for an air mail letter
für einen Einschreibebrief	*führ ay-nuhn ayn-shRay-buh-bReef*	for a registered letter

continues

continued

German	Pronunciation	English
für eine Eilpost	*führR ay-nuh ayl-post*	for a special delivery
für einen Eilbrief	*führR ay-nuhn ayl-bReef*	for an express letter

Here are a few more useful phrases:

Ich möchte diesen Brief (per Luftpost, per Eilpost) verschicken.
iH möH-tuh dee-zuhn bReef (peR looft-post, peR ayl-post) feR-shi-kuhn
I would like to send this letter (by air mail, special delivery).

Ich möchte dieses Paket per Nachnahme schicken.
iH möH-tuh dee-zuhs pah-keyt peR nahCH-nah-muh shi-kuhn
I would like to send this package C.O.D.

Wieviel wiegt dieser Brief?
vee-feel veekt dee-zuhR bReef
How much does this letter weigh?

Wann wird der Brief ankommen?
vAn viRt deyR bReef An-ko-muhn
When will the letter arrive?

Wie lange dauert es, bis der Brief ankommt?
vee lAn-guh dou-eRt es, bis deyR bReef An-komt
How long will it take for the letter to arrive?

When You Want to Send a Telegram

Of course, there are times when a letter just doesn't get there fast enough. What do you do? When time is of the essence, send a telegram.

Ich möchte ein Telegramm senden.
iH möH-tuh ayn tey-ley-gRAm zen-duhn
I would like to send a telegram.

Wie hoch ist der Tarif pro Wort?
vee hoCH ist deyR tA-Reef pRo voRt
How much is the rate per word?

Könnte ich bitte ein (Antrags) Formular bekommen?
kön-tuh iH bi-tuh ayn (An-tRahks) foR-mew-lahR
buh-ko-muhn
May I please have a form?

Wo gibt es die Formulare?
voh gipt es dee foR-mew-lah-Ruh
Where are the forms?

Sagen Sie mal...

The postal service in Germany also provides phone service.
Tell the postal worker behind the counter that you'd like
to make a long-distance call and he or she will indicate
which phone booth is available. You pay (cash only) after
the call. It's generally considerably less expensive than
making calls from hotels, or even from the gray phone
booths you'll see along city streets.

When You Write in German, You *schreibt*

When you're filling out forms at the post office, you may
have some trouble figuring out what goes into which tiny
bureaucratic-looking box. To ask one of the postal workers
where you should write what information, use the strong
verb *schreiben* (*shRay-buhn*), to write.

Table 14.5 The Verb schreiben

English	Singular	Plural
I write/we write	ich schreibe *iH shRay-buh*	wir schreiben *veeR shRay-buhn*
you write	du schreibst *dew shRaypst*	ihr schreibt *eeR shRaypt*
(Formal)	Sie schreiben *zee shRay-buhn*	Sie schreiben *zee shRay-buhn*
he, she, it writes/they write	er, sie, es schreibt *eR, zee, es shRaypt*	sie schreiben *zee shRay-buhn*

Speaking of writing, you'll also be doing a lot reading—of signs, of forms, of your own letters, and of other people's letters. The strong verb *lesen* (*ley-zuhn*), to read, will help you express exactly what kind of reading you are doing.

Table 14.6 The Verb lesen

English	Singular	Plural
I read/we read	ich lese *iH ley-zuh*	wir lesen *veeR ley-zuhn*
you read	du liest *dew leest*	ihr lest *eeR leest*
(Formal)	Sie lesen *zee ley-zuhn*	Sie lesen *zee ley-zuhn*
he, she, it reads/they read	er, sie, es liest *eR, zee, es leest*	sie lesen *zee ley-zuhn*

Reading in German

Have you been glancing at German magazines and newspapers whenever you pass a newsstand? Why don't you buy one? One of the best ways to progress in your reading skills is to do just that: Read. Table 14.7 provides you with a list of things you can read when you are in Germany.

Table 14.7 Things to Read

German	Pronunciation	English
die Anzeige	*dee an-zay-guh*	ad
das Buch	*dAs bewH*	book
der Fahrplan	*deyR fahR-plAn*	train/bus schedule
die Speisekarte	*dee shpay-zuh-kAR-tuh*	menu
die Zeitschrift	*dee tsayt-shRift*	magazine
die Zeitung	*dee tsay-toonk*	newspaper
die Quittung	*dee kvi-toonk*	receipt
der Roman	*deyR roh-mahn*	novel
das Schild	*dAs shilt*	sign
die Warnung	*dee vAR-noonk*	warning

Do You Know the Difference Between *wissen* and *kennen*?

Smart people know everything and wise people know that they don't know anything at all. Whether you know everything or nothing, one thing you'll have to know is how to use the verbs *wissen* (*vi-suhn*), *kennen* (*ke-nuhn*), and *können* (*kö-nuhn*). All three verbs express "to know." You've already conjugated *können*, a modal auxiliary verb, in Chapter 9. Here, you conjugate *wissen* and *kennen*.

IS There a Difference?

When do you use *wissen*, when do you use *kennen,* and when do you use *können*? *Wissen* is used primarily to express knowledge of facts and, except when used with indefinite pronouns, is usually followed by a subordinate clause: *Ich weiß, wo der nächste Briefkasten ist* (*iH vays vo deyR näH-stuh bReef-kah-stuhn ist*). *Kennen* is used to express that you know (or are acquainted with): people, places, things, ideas, and, less frequently than *wissen* and *kennen*, to indicate that you are skilled at something. It is generally followed by a "one-word" direct object: *Ich kenne den Briefträger nicht.* Remember that *können* is a modal and often is used with another verb that appears at the end of the sentence: *Ich kann den Brief morgen abschicken.*

Ich weiß, was er meint.
iH vays, vAs eR maynt
I know what he means.

Weißt du wie man Auto fahrt?
vayst dew vee mAn ou-toh fahRt
Do you know how one drives a car?

Sie kennt die Königin von England.
zee kent dee köh-nih-gin fon eng-lAnt
She knows the Queen of England.

Kennst du dieses Lied?
kenst dew dee-suhs leet
Do you know this song?

Wir können Deutsch sprechen.
veeR kö-nuhn doytsh spre-Huhn
We know how to speak German.

Table 14.8 The Verb wissen

English	Singular	Plural
I know/we know	ich weiß *iH vays*	wir wissen *veeR vi-suhn*
you know	du weißt *dew vayst*	ihr wißt *eeR vist*
(Formal)	Sie wissen *zee vi-suhn*	Sie wissen *zee vi-suhn*
he, she it knows/they know	er, sie, es weiß *eR, zee, es vays*	sie wissen *zee vi-suhn*

Table 14.9 The Verb kennen

English	Singular	Plural
I know/we know	ich kenne *iH ke-nuh*	wir kennen *veeR ke-nuhn*
you know	du kennst *dew kenst*	ihr kennt *eeR kent*
(Formal)	Sie kennen *zee ke-nuhn*	Sie kennen *zee ke-nuhn*
he, she, it knows/they know	er, sie, es kennt *eR, zee, es kent*	sie kennen *zee ke-nuhn*

Chapter 15

Spending Your
Deutschmarks and Pfennigs

In This Chapter

➤ Banking terms

➤ Cashing traveler's checks and exchanging money

➤ Renting apartments and houses

➤ Rooms, furnishings, amenities, and appliances

➤ Speaking in the subjunctive mood

It's time for you to learn how to deal with money in a foreign country. If you're involved in business, many of the terms you are introduced to in this chapter will be of use to you. Or you may want to rent a house or apartment. We'll tell you how to do that as well.

Get Me to the Bank on Time

Hotels, restaurants, and banks—these are the places where you will probably spend a good deal of your time when you travel. Banks will be of particular importance to you, because sooner or later, you'll probably need to exchange money, to cash traveler's checks, or to receive a cash advance on one of your credit cards. If you're planning to reside for an extended period of time in a German-speaking country, you may even want to take out a loan to set up a business, purchase real estate, invest in the stock market, or open a checking account.

Talking Like a Banker

If you need to do anything involving your friendly local banker, you'll have to acquaint yourself with the banking terms in Table 15.1.

Table 15.1   Mini-Dictionary of Banking Terms

German	Pronunciation	English
abheben	*Ap-hey-buhn*	withdraw
ausfüllen	*ous-fü-luhn*	fill out
leihen	*lay-huhn*	borrow
das Bankkonto	*dAs bAnk-kon-toh*	bank account
das Bargeld	*dAs bahR-gelt*	cash
das Darlehen	*dAs dahR-ley-huhn*	loan
das Einkommen	*dAs ayn-ko-muhn*	revenue
das Geldwechselbüro	*dAs gelt-ve-ksel-büh-Roh*	money exchange bureau
das Kontobuch	*dAs kon-toh-bewCH*	bankbook
das Scheckbuch	*dAs shek-bewCH*	checkbook
das Sparkonto	*dAs shpAR-kon-toh*	savings account
das Wechselgeld	*dAs ve-ksel-gelt*	change (coins)
der (Kassen) Schalter	*deyR (kA-suhn) shAl-tuhR*	(teller's) window
der Angestellte	*deyR An-guh-shtel-tuh*	employee

German	Pronunciation	English
der Ankauf	*deyR An-kouf*	purchase
der Bankautomat	*deyR bAnk-ou-toh-maht*	automatic teller machine
der Bankbeamte/ die Bankbeamtin	*deyR bAnk-bey-Am-tuh/ dee bAnk-bey-Am-tin*	bank employee
der Bankdirektor	*deyR bAnk-dee-Rek-tohR*	bank manager
der Einzahlungsbeleg	*deyR ayn-tsah-looks-bey-leyk*	deposit slip
der Geldfluß	*deyR gelt-floos*	cash flow
der Geldschein	*deyR gelt-shayn*	bill
der Kassierer/ die Kassiererin	*deyR kA-see-RuhR/ dee kA-see-Ruh-Rin*	teller
der Kontostand	*deyR kon-toh-shtAnt*	balance
der Reisescheck	*deyR Ray-zuh-shek*	traveler's check
der Verkauf	*deyR feR-kouf*	sale
der Wechselkurs	*deyR ve-ksel-kooRs*	exchange rate
die Abhebung	*dee Ap-hey-boong*	withdrawal
die Abzahlung	*dee Ap-zah-loong*	installment payment
die Anzahlung	*dee An-zah-loong*	down payment
die Einzahlung	*dee ayn-tsah-loong*	deposit
die Filiale	*dee fi-lee-ah-luh*	branch
die Hypothek	*dee hüh-poh-teyk*	mortgage
die Münze	*dee mün-tsuh*	coin
die Quittung	*dee kvi-toong*	receipt
die Ratenzahlung	*dee Rah-tuhn-tsah-loong*	installment plan
die Restzahlung	*dee Rest-tsah-loong*	final payment
die Schulden	*dee shool-duhn*	debt
die Überweisung	*dee üh-buhR-vay-zoong*	transfer
die Überziehung	*dee üh-buhR-tsee-hoong*	overdraft

continues

Table 15.1 Continued

German	Pronunciation	English
die Unterschrift	*dee oon-tuhR-shRift*	signature
die Zahlung	*dee tsah-loong*	payment
ein überberzogener Scheck (m.)	*ayn üh-buhR-tsoh-guh-nuhR shek*	an overdrawn check
einzahlen	*ayn-tsah-luhn*	to deposit
kurzfristig	*kooRts-fRis-tiH*	short term
langfristig	*lAnk-fRis-tiH*	long term
das Konto überziehen	*dAs kon-toh üh-buhR-tsee-huhn*	to overdraft
sparen	*shpah-Ruhn*	save
überweisen	*üh-buhR-vay-zuhn*	transfer
unterschreiben	*oon-tuhR-shRay-buhn*	sign (to)
verleihen	*feR-lay-huhn*	to loan
wechseln	*ve-ksuhln*	change (transaction)

Exchanging Your Money

In Germany, money can be exchanged at *Wechselstuben* (*vek-suhl-shtew-buhn*), or money exchange booths, at airports, and train stations. The *Deutsche Verkehrs-Kredit Bank* has branches in train stations that stay open until 6 p.m. Your best bet, however, is to exchange money at one of the larger branches of a bank in cities (you may have some trouble in the smaller towns) where the exchange rates are higher and the commission is lower. Most hotels also exchange money, but their rates are a complete rip-off, really—*ein totaler Nepp*. It's hardly even worth mentioning them.

If it's traveler's checks you're looking to exchange, you can do this in the same places you might go to exchange money: Banks, money exchange booths, and post offices.

You'll have trouble getting anyone to accept traveler's checks as direct payment.

Then—are you ready?—once again, there's the miraculous German post office. In addition to selling stamps, sending packages, and connecting you with long-distance operators, the bureaucratic angels in the German post office also will change your money for you, which is something you may want to keep in mind if you're cashless in the late afternoon: Post offices stay open until 6 p.m.

Achtung!

Although many establishments in Germany do accept credit cards, plastic is a less widespread phenomenon in Germany than it is in the United States. Be sure that you see the imprimatur of your credit card company on the window or menu of the establishment where you're about to eat—otherwise you may be washing dishes till the banks open at 9:00 a.m.

Accessing Your Money

If you plan to settle down in Germany, prepare yourself for the banking experience that awaits you by familiarizing yourself with the following phrases (the phrases you use will depend on whether you're going to exchange money, make a deposit or a withdrawal, open a checking or savings account, or apply for a loan).

Wie sind ihre Öffnungszeiten?
vee sint ee-Ruh öf-nooks-tsay-tuhn
What are the banking hours?

Ich möchte…
iH möH-tuh
I would like…

>…eine Einzahlung machen
>*ay-nuh ayn-tsah-loong mA-CHuhn*
>…to make a deposit

>…eine Abhebung machen
>*ay-nuh Ap-hey-boong mA-CHuhn*
>…to make a withdrawal

>…eine Zahlung machen
>*ay-nuh tsah-loong mA-CHuhn*
>…to make a payment

>…einen Scheck einlösen
>*ay-nuhn shek ayn-löh-zuhn*
>…to cash a check

>…ein Konto eröffnen
>*ayn kon-toh eR-öf-nuhn*
>…to open an account

>…ein Konto schließen
>*ayn kon-toh shlee-suhn*
>…to close an account

>…etwas Geld wechseln
>*etvAs gelt ve-ksuhln*
>…to change some money

Wie hoch ist der heutige Wechselkurs?
vee hoCH ist deyR hoy-ti-guh ve-ksuhl-kooRs
How high is today's exchange rate?

Haben Sie einen Bankeautomaten?
hah-buhn zee ay-nuhn bAnk-ou-toh-mahtuhn
Do you have an automatic teller machine?

Wie benutzt man ihn?
vee buh-nootst mAn een
How does one use it?

Wie hoch ist die Zinsrate?
vee hoCH ist dee tsins-Rah-tuh
What is the interest rate?

Sagen Sie mal...

One Deutschmark (DM) consists of 100 Pfennig (pf). Use cardinal numbers to talk about coins. Die Pfennige, (*dee pfe-ni-guh*) coins are divided into 1, 2, 5, 10, and 50 pf coins. Die Deutsche Mark (*dee doy-chuh mARk*) come in these denominations: 5, 10, 20, 50, 100, 200, 500, and 1,000 DM. In Switzerland, the currency is Franken, (*fRAn-kuhn*), divided into 100 Rappen, (*RA-puhn*); in Austria, it is Schillinge, (*shi-lin-guh*), divided into 100 Groschen, (*gRo-shuhn*).

I'd Like to Rent a Castle, Please

You should be prepared to read and understand the apartments for rent and houses for sale sections of the *Zeitung* and be able to speak with real estate agents about what is available to rent or buy. Table 15.2 helps you learn the vocabulary you'll need to describe your dream *Schloß* (*shlos*).

Table 15.2   The House, the Apartment, the Rooms

German	Pronunciation	English
das Arbeitszimmer	*dAs AR-bayts-tsi-muhR*	study
das Badezimmer	*dAs bah-duh-tsi-muhR*	bathroom
das Dach	*dAs dACH*	roof

continues

Table 15.2 Continued

German	Pronunciation	English
das Dachgeschoβ	*dAs dACH-guh-shos*	attic
das Erdgeschoβ	*dAs eRt-guh-shos*	ground floor
das Eβzimmer	*dAs es-tsi-muhR*	dining room
das Fenster	*dAs fen-stuhR*	window
das Geschoβ	*dAs guh-shos*	floor (story)
das Schlafzimmer	*dAs shlahf-tsi-muhR*	bedroom
das Treppenhaus	*dAs tRe-puhn-hous*	staircase
das Wohnzimmer	*dAs vohn-tsi-muhR*	living room
der Abstellraum	*deyR Ap-shtel-Roum*	storage room
der Aufzug	*deyR ouf-tsewk*	elevator
der Besitzer	*deyR buh-zit-suhR*	owner
der Fuβboden	*deyR fews-boh-duhn*	floor
der Hinterhof	*deyR hin-tuhR-hohf*	backyard
der Innenhof	*deyR i-nuhn-hohf*	courtyard
der Kamin	*deyR kah-meen*	fireplace
der Keller	*deyR ke-luhR*	basement
der Mieter	*deyR mee-tuhR*	tenant
der Mietvertrag	*deyR meet-veR-tRahk*	lease
der Portier	*deyR poR-tee-eR*	doorman
der Vermieter	*deyR feR-mee-tuhR*	landlord
der Wandschrank	*deyR vAnt-shRAnk*	closet
die Decke	*dee de-kuh*	ceiling
die Dusche	*dee dew-shuh*	shower
die elektrische Heizung	*dee ey-lek-tRi-shuh hay-tsoong*	electric heating
die Gasheizung	*dee gahs-hay-tsoong*	gas heating
die Instandhaltung	*dee in-shtAnt-hAl-toong*	maintenance
die Klimaanlage	*dee klee-mah-An-lah-guh*	air conditioning

German	Pronunciation	English
die Küche	*dee kü-Huh*	kitchen
die Miete	*dee mee-tuh*	rent
die Sauna	*dee zou-nah*	sauna
die Terrasse	*dee te-RA-suh*	terrace
die Wand	*dee vAnt*	wall
die Waschküche	*dee vAsh-kü-Huh*	laundry room
die Wohnung	*dee voh-noong*	apartment

How to Explain What You're Looking for

Do you want to rent an apartment?

Ich suche...
iH zew-Chuh
I'm looking for...

>...einen Immobilienmakler (m.)
>*ay-nuhn i-moh-bee-lee-uhn-mAk-luhR*
>...a real estate agency

>...den Anzeigenteil
>*den An-tsay-guhn-tayl*
>...the advertisement section

>...den Anzeigenteil für Immobilien
>*deyn An-tsay-guhn-tayl fühR i-moh-bee-lee-uhn*
>...the real estate advertising section

Ich möchte...mieten.
iH möH-tuh...mee-tuhn
I would like to rent (buy)...

>...eine Wohnung
>*ay-nuh voh-noong*
>...an apartment

...eine Eigentumswohnung
ay-nuh ay-guhn-tewms-voh-noong
...a condominium

Wie hoch ist die Miete?
vee hohCH ist dee mee-tuh
What is the rent?

Wie teuer ist die Instandhaltung der Wohnung
(des Hauses)?
vee toy-uhR ist dee in-shtAnt-hAl-toon deyR voh-noong
(des hou-zuhs)
How much is the maintenance of the apartment
(house)?

Wie hoch sind die monatlichen Zahlungen?
vee hohCH zint dee moh-nAt-li-Huhn tsah-loon-guhn
How much are the monthly payments?

Muß ich eine Kaution hintelassen?
moos iH ay-nuh kou-tsee-ohn hin-tuhR-lA-suhn
Do I have to leave a deposit?

Furnishing Your New Home

Table 15.3 gives you a head start on the furniture and
accessories you may not know you need until you really
start to miss them.

Table 15.3   Furniture and Accessories

German	Pronunciation	English
das Bett	*dAs bet*	bed
das Bücherregal	*dAs bü-HuhR-Rey-gahl*	bookshelf
das Eisfach	*dAs ays-fACH*	freezer
der Fernseher	*deyR feRn-zey-huhR*	television
der Kühlschrank	*deyR kühl-shRAnk*	refrigerator
der Ofen	*deyR o-fuhn*	oven

German	Pronunciation	English
der Sessel	*deyR ze-suhl*	armchair
der Stuhl	*deyR shtewl*	chair
der Teppich	*deyR tey-piH*	carpet
der Tisch	*deyR tish*	table
der Trochner	*deyR tRoH-nuhR*	dryer
die elektrischen Küchengeräte	*dee e-lek-tRi-shuhn kü-Huhn-guh-Rä-tuh*	kitchen appliances
die Gardinen	*dee gAR-dee-nuhn*	curtains
die Kommode	*dee ko-moh-duh*	dresser
die Möbel (pl.)	*dee m'öh-buhl*	furniture
die Spühlmaschine	*dee shpühl-mA-shee-nuh*	dishwasher
die Uhr	*dee ewR*	clock

Speaking of the Future

If you're planning to rent property, the first thing you're going to have to do is learn how to express your plans in the future tense. There are a number of ways of to do this.

Was haben Sie gesagt?

Future Tense   To form the future tense, use the present tense of the auxiliary verb *werden* with the infinitive of the verb.

The Future Tense

To express the future in German colloquial speech, the present tense is often used with a future implication. This also is done in English, though not as commonly. If someone asks you what you are going to do later in the day, you could say, *Go home, I guess. Go to bed. After that, sleep.* Another way of speaking in the future is by using the future tense. To form the future tense, use the present tense of the auxiliary verb *werden* (*veR-duhn*), which means "to become" with the infinitive of the verb:

> subject + conjugated present tense of *werden* + the infinitive of the verb

Table 15.4 conjugates the verb *kaufen* for you in the future tense.

Table 15.4 Kaufen in the Future Tense

English	Singular	Plural
I will buy/ we will buy	ich werde kaufen *iH veR-duh kou-fuhn*	wir werden kaufen *veeR veR-duhn kou-fuhn*
you will buy	du wirst kaufen *dew veeRst kou-fuhn*	ihr werdet kaufen *eeR veR-det kou-fuh*
(Formal)	Sie werden kaufen *zee veR-duhn kou-fuhn*	Sie werden kaufen *zee veR-duhn kou-fuhn*
he she, it will buy/ they will buy	er, sie, es wird kaufen *eR, zee, es virt kou-fuhn*	sie werden kaufen *zee veR-duhn kou-fuhn*

Getting Subjunctive

If you're not sure whether you're going to get everything done, you will probably want to use the subjunctive mood. In an ideal world, you would never have to use this mood—you would make a list of things to do and do them. You would put on your jogging shoes and step outside and run four miles. You would clean your apartment;

you would write letters to your mother. Unfortunately, as much as you would like to do things, as much as you *should* do them, you don't always get them done. Thank goodness for the subjunctive mood.

A Subjunctive Mood

German has separate forms for verbs that are in the subjunctive mood, forms that are used to express wishes or contrary-to-fact statements. But German, and English, have an easy way to form the subjunctive. You just use "would" (the subjunctive form of "will") and the infinitive of a verb, for example, "would rent" or "würde mieten." Here is the basic formula you should use to form sentences in the subjunctive:

Subject + *würde* (conjugated to agree with subject) + infinitive

Wir würden ein großes, altes Schloß mieten.

You can use this formula with most verbs. You will find *werden* conjugated in the subjunctive in Table 15.5 with the verb *mieten* (*mee-tuhn*), to rent. Use this conjugation of *werden* with every verb you use to form the subjunctive.

Here is the basic formula you should use to form sentences in the subjunctive:

Subject + *werden* conjugated in the subjunctive + infinitive of the verb

Table 15.5   Mieten in the Subjunctive Mood

English	Singular	Plural
I will rent/ we will rent	ich würde mieten *iH veR-duh mee-tuhn*	wir würden mieten *veeR mee-tuhn*
you will rent	du würdest mieten *dew vüR-duhst mee-tuhn*	ihr würdet mieten *eeR veR-det mee-tuhn*

continues

Table 15.5 Continued

English	Singular	Plural
(Formal)	Sie würden mieten *zee veR-duhn mee-tuhn*	Sie würden mieten *zee veR-duhn mee-tuhn*
he, she, it will rent/ they will rent	er, sie, es würde mieten *eR, zee, es vüR-duh mee-tuhn*	sie würden mieten *zee veR-duhn mee-tuhn*

Enjoy!

Was würden Sie am liebsten tun in Deutschland? (What would you like most to do in Germany?) It's all up to you! How about: *Ich würde am liebsten einen BMW kaufen.* Now, you don't need us to translate that for you, do you? We know you're good to go. Have fun!

Appendix A

Pronunciation Guide

Letter(s)	Symbol	English Example	German Example
Vowels			
a (short)	*A*	Close to modern	Mann
a (long)	*ah*	father	Lage
e (short, stressed)	*e*	bed	Bett
e (short, unstressed)	*uh*	ago	Bitte
e (long)	*ey*	Close to hey	Weg
i (short)	*i*	wind	Wind
i (long)	*ee*	see	wir
o (short)	*o*	lord	Ort
o (long)	*oh*	Close to snow	Verbot
u (short)	*oo*	shook	Mutter
u (long)	*ew*	stew	Versuch
Modified Vowels			
ä (short)	*ä*	fair	Stärke

continues

continued

Letter(s)	Symbol	English Example	German Example
		Modified Vowels (Continued)	
ä (long)	*äh*	Close to f*a*te	B*ä*r
ö (short)	*ö*	Close to f*u*r	L*ö*ffel
ö (long)	*öh*	Close to h*u*rt	sch*ö*n
ü (short)	*ü*	Close to f*oo*d	Gl*ü*ck
ü (long)	*üh*	Close to f*oo*d	l*ü*gen
		Diphthongs	
ai, ei	*ay*	*I*	Bl*ei*stift
au	*ou*	c*ou*ch	Fr*au*
äu, eu	*oy*	t*oy*	h*eu*te
		Consonants That Differ from English	
b	*b*	*b*ig	*B*leistift
	p	*p*ipe	o*b*wohl
c	*ts*	ba*ts*	*C*esar
	k	*k*iller	*C*omputer
ch	*H*	Close to *h*uman	i*ch*
	CH	No equivalent	su*ch*en
	k	*ch*aracter	*Ch*aracter
	sh	*sh*ape	*Ch*ef
chs	*x*	fo*x*	Fu*chs*
d	*d*	*d*og	*D*ach
	t	*t*ime	Wan*d*
g	*g*	*g*ood	*g*roß
	k	*k*itten	We*g*
	j	*j*eans	Massa*g*e
h	*h*	*h*ouse	*H*eimat

Letter(s)	Symbol	English Example	German Example
j	*y*	*y*es	*j*a
kn	*kn*	No equivalent	*Kn*eipe
pf	*pf*	No equivalent	*Pf*eife
ph	*f*	*ph*oto	*Ph*oto
ps	*ps*	*ps*st!	*Ps*eudonym
ng	*ng*	sli*ng*	Schli*ng*e
qu	*kv*	No equivalent	*Qu*atch
r	*R*	No equivalent	*r*eich
s	*z*	*z*ero	*S*uppe
	s	mou*s*e	Gla*s*
β, ss	*s*	*s*alt	Stra*β*e, Ma*ss*e
sch	*sh*	*sh*ape	*Sch*atten
sp	*shp*	No equivalent	*sp*ielen
st	*sht*	No equivalent	*St*urm
	st	*st*ate	La*st*
tsch	*tch*	sni*tch*	deu*tsch*
v	*f*	*f*ather	*V*ater
	v	*v*oice	*V*ase
w	*v*	*v*ast	*w*ichtig
z	*ts*	ca*ts*	*Z*eug

Common German Idiomatic Expressions

The German expression for being lucky is *Schwein haben* (*shvayn hah-buhn*) which, literally translated, means "to have pig." Don't be too quick to take offense at something that sounds like an insult; it may be an idiomatic expression.

What Are Idiomatic Expressions, Anyway?

Idiomatic expressions are speech forms or expressions that cannot be understood by literal translation—they must be learned and memorized along with their meanings.

Idiomatic Expressions in German

The following table lists a few of the most commonly used German idiomatic expressions (along with their corresponding English meanings).

Common German Idiomatic Expressions

Idiom	Pronunciation	Meaning
Er tickt nicht richtig.	*eR tikt niHt RiH-tiH*	He's not all there. (Literally, he isn't ticking.)
Ich habe die Nase vol.	*iH hah-buh dee nah-zuh fol*	I've had enough. (Literally, my nose is full.)
Jetzt geht es um die Wurst.	*yetst geyt es oom dee vooRst*	Now or never. (Literally, now it gets about the sausage.)
Nimm mich nicht auf den Arm.	*nim miH niHt ouf deyn ARm*	Don't pull my leg. (Literally, don't take me in your arms.)
Sie hat nicht alle Tassen im Schrank.	*zee hAt niHt A-luh tA-suhn im shRAnk*	She's missing a few marbles. (Lilterally, all her cups aren't in the cupboard.)
Ich bin verrückt nach Dir.	*iH bin fe-Rükt nACH deeR*	I'm crazy about you.
Aus tiefstem Herzen.	*ous teef-stuhm heR-tsuhn*	From the bottom of my heart. (Literally, out of the deepest heart.)
Ich drücke Dir die Daumen.	*iH dRü-kuh deeR dee dou-muhn*	I cross my fingers for you. (Literally, I press my thumbs for you.)

Saying the Right Thing

You know the saying, the early bird gets the worm. Do you know what it means? Neither do we. Still, sayings are everywhere in language, embodying familiar truths and generally accepted beliefs in colorful, expressive language. Here are a few German sayings and the English counterparts.

Sagen Sie mal...

Literally translated, the German slang expression *Das ist mir Wurst* (*dAs ist meeR vooRst*) means "That's sausage to me." Although a great many Germans appear to love their sausage, this expression is used to show indifference. The idiomatic equivalent would be *Das ist mir egal* (*das ist meeR ey-gahl*), which means "It's the same to me."

Sayings

German Saying	Pronunciation	English Equivalent
Wer zuerst kommt, mahlt zuerst.	*veyR tsew-eRst komt, mahlt tsew-eRst*	The early bird gets the worm.
Was ich nicht weis, macht mich nicht heiß.	*vas iH niHt ways, mAHt miH niHt hays*	What I don't know can't hurt me.
Wer zuletzt lacht, lacht am Besten.	*veyR tsew-letst lAHt, lAHt Am bes-tuhn*	He who laughs last, laughs best.
Wer lügt, der stiehlt.	*veyR lühkt, deyR shteelt*	He who lies, steals.
Iß, was gar ist, trink, was klar ist, sprich was wahr ist.	*is, vAs gahR ist, tRink, vAs klahR ist, shpriH vAs vahR ist*	Eat what is cooked, drink what is clear, speak what is true.

Index

Symbols

β, 11
¨ (umlaut), 4-6, 8-9

A

a, pronunciation, 7
ä, pronunciation, 8
a/an/one, *see* indefinite articles
accomodations, hotels, 97-99
accusative case, 39
    object pronouns, 132
activities, 140
adages, *see* sayings
address, 67
    formal, 46
    in greeting, 64-65
    informal, 46
adjectives
    cognates, perfect, 22
    colors, 129-130
    comparative, 171-174
    declension of, 77-82
        mixed, 81-82
        strong, 80
        weak, 78-79

irregular, 178
positive form, 171
possessive, 74-76
stark (strong), 172
superlative, 171-172
versus adverbs, 174
adverbs, 174-178
    categories of, 177-178
    comparative, 171-172
    irregular, 178
    non-adjectival, 176
    positive form, 171
    stark (strong), 172
    superlative, 171-172
    versus adjectives, 174
ai, pronunciation, 9
airplane travel, 83-84
airport, 84-85
always plural nouns, 36
am (on), days of the week, 109
amenities, hotel, 98-99
answering questions, 60-61
    dates, 113
    negative phrases, 60-61
    seit, 184
apartments, 219-222
articles
    cities, 66
    countries, 66

U–V